Saltwater Sport Fish of the Gulf

FIELD GUIDE

by Dave Bosanko

Adventure Publications
Cambridge, Minnesota

ACKNOWLEDGEMENTS

Special thanks to Dr. Kenneth L. Krysko of the Florida Museum of Natural History, University of Florida.

Edited by Brett Ortler

Cover and book design by Jonathan Norberg

Illustration credits by artist and page number:

Cover illustrations: Red Snapper (main) by Julie Martinez; Sheepshead (upper front cover and back cover) by Carlyn Iverson

Carlyn Iverson: 44, 88, 122, 186 **MyFWC.com/fishing:** 15 **Duane Raver/ USFWS:** 42, 48, 62, 176 **Julie Martinez:** all other illustrations

10 9 8 7 6 5 4

Saltwater Sport Fish of the Gulf Field Guide
Copyright © 2010 by Dave Bosanko
Published by Adventure Publications, an imprint of AdventureKEEN
330 Garfield Street South
Cambridge, Minnesota 55008
(800) 678-7006
www.adventurepublications.net
Printed in China
ISBN 978-1-59193-254-3 (pbk.)

TABLE OF CONTENTS

Atlantic Cutlassfish Family ————————
   Atlantic Cutlassfish . . . . 35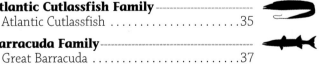

Barracuda Family ————————
   Great Barracuda 37

3

ABOUT THE GULF OF MEXICO

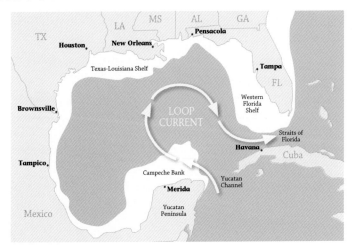

The Gulf of Mexico is a large ocean basin that is mainly enclosed by the North American continent. It is bound to the west by Mexico and the Yucatan Peninsula, to the north by the US Gulf Coast states, and to the east by Florida. The island of Cuba is located in the southeastern portion of the Gulf, and it borders the two primary gateways to the rest of the Atlantic: the Yucatan Channel and the Straits of Florida.

The Yucatan Channel

The Yucatan Channel is located between Cuba and the Yucatan Peninsula. Here the Caribbean Current enters the Gulf and makes a clockwise loop up to the Texas-Louisiana coast; it then flows along Mississippi, Alabama and Florida before exiting between Florida and Cuba. The Loop Current is weak and is often overcome by local weather conditions. Some minor currents in the western Gulf offshore of Texas and Mexico circle counterclockwise.

The Straits of Florida

The Florida Straits is the area between Florida and Cuba where water leaves the Gulf and flows into the Atlantic. The Straits are fed by the weak Loop Current that brings nutrient-rich water from the cooler northern Gulf. The Straits are always warm and the only truly tropical waters of the Gulf. Many warmwater species that occasionally, if ever, make it to the northern Gulf are persistent residents of the Florida Straits.

The Continental Shelf

On average, the Gulf of Mexico is relatively shallow, as large portions of it sit on the continental shelf. A transitional zone between dry land and deep water, the continental shelf runs along the perimeter of the Gulf and ranges from a few feet to 60 feet deep. The shelf is narrowest in Mexico, then begins to widen northeast of Brownsville, Texas. In the western Gulf, the widest part of the continental shelf is found between Houston and New Orleans and is referred to as the Texas-Louisiana Shelf.

The continental shelf is at its widest along Alabama and Florida. Eventually, it gives way to an area of deep valleys and ridges that ranges from 60 to 800 feet deep. The edge of the Western Florida Shelf is not nearly as rugged, and it extends relatively smoothly out to the central Gulf. The central Gulf is a deep basin ranging from 1,000 to 12,000 feet deep.

With all these varied habitats, all of which are fed by warm nutrient-rich currents, the Gulf of Mexico is one of the premier fishing grounds in the world. From the many bays and estuaries and all the way out to the blue water of the open ocean, the sport fishing opportunities are limitless. This book is designed to help you identify and catch the most common fish in this vast expanse of water.

Texas

Texas has a thousand miles of Gulf shoreline, most of which is protected by barrier islands. There is great offshore fishing for Cobia, Snappers and Billfish, but the large, protected bays are the real gems of Texas saltwater fishing. From the huge Laguna Madre to Corpus Christi Bay, some of the best trout, flounder and Red Drum fishing in the Gulf can be found in Texas. Many specialized techniques for finding and catching the "big three" have been perfected for these shallow, windy bays. In these Texan bays, it's also not uncommon to tangle with a hundred-pound stingray.

Louisiana

Offshore fishing in Louisiana is dominated by oil rigs. As ugly as these things are, they are great for attracting fish. Redfish and trout can be caught around the shallow-water rigs, Dolphin and Sailfish near deepwater rigs and everything else in between. Some of the best Cobia fishing in the Gulf can be found around midwater rigs. Inshore, the redfish is the king of Louisiana sport fishing. Louisiana has millions of acres of coastal salt marshes that are prime redfish habitat, but this water can also provide some fine fishing for trout, sheepshead and flounder.

Mississippi

The primary marine fishing in Mississippi occurs around the large islands found just offshore in the Mississippi Sound. The Mississippi Sound is extensive, so deepwater fishing expeditions often involve long boat rides, but can be very productive. Mississippi's extensive beaches are the often overlooked jewels of the state's saltwater fishing. Wading and surf casting the beaches produces good catches of whiting, flounder and the occasional shark.

Alabama

Alabama has the least amount of Gulf shoreline of any of the Gulf States but some of the best fishing. Offshore, there are good natural and man-made reefs that provide excellent snapper and grouper fishing. These reefs also draw in many of the deepwater fish during the warmer months and are often real hotspots for mackerel. Inshore, Mobile Bay is a prime redfish, flounder and trout water. The Alabama beaches should not be forgotten either; surf fishing is good there year around.

Florida

Florida has the most coastline of all the Gulf States and perhaps the widest variety of habitat, as it is home to everything from cool northern waters to subtropical keys. The northern waters are famous for redfish and trout, whereas the Keys are well known for Bonefish, Permit, snook and Tarpon. In the north, it's a long way out to blue water, but in the south the deepwater fish almost come in to shore. All along the Florida coast, bridge and pier fishing can be excellent.

FISH ANATOMY

Fish Terminology

Throughout *Saltwater Sport Fish of the Gulf* we use basic biological and fisheries management terms that refer to physical characteristics or conditions of fish and their environment, such as dorsal fin or turbid water. For your convenience, these are listed and defined in the Glossary (pp. 188–191), along with other handy fish-related terms and their definitions.

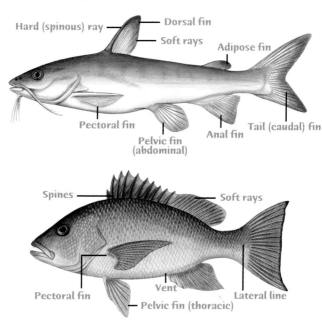

Hard (spinous) ray
Dorsal fin
Soft rays
Adipose fin
Pectoral fin
Pelvic fin (abdominal)
Anal fin
Tail (caudal) fin

Spines
Soft rays
Pectoral fin
Vent
Pelvic fin (thoracic)
Lateral line

Understanding such terminology will help you make sense of reports on state and federal research, fish population surveys, management plans and other important fisheries documents.

To identify fish, you will need to know a few basic terms that apply to fins and their locations.

Fins are made up of bony structures that support a membrane. There are three kinds of bony structures in fins. **Soft rays** are flexible fin supports that are sometimes branched. **Spines** are stiff, often sharp, supports that are not jointed. **Hard rays** are stiff, pointed, barbed structures that can be raised or lowered. Sea catfish are famous for their very sharp, hard rays that lock into place; these are often mistakenly called spines. Fins are named by their position on the fish. The **dorsal fin** is on top of the fish along the midline. Dorsal fins are made up of soft rays and hard spines, and these can be joined as one fin or separated. A few fish have another fin on their back called an **adipose fin**. This is a small, fleshy protuberance located between the dorsal fin and the tail and is distinctive of sea catfish.

The **pectoral fins** are on each side of the fish near the gills. The **anal fin** is located along the midline on the fish's bottom or ventral side. There is also a paired set of fins on the bottom of the fish called the **pelvic fins**. Pelvic fins can be in the **thoracic position** just below the pectoral fins or farther back on the stomach in the **abdominal position**. The tail is known as the **caudal fin**.

Eyes—In general, fish have good eyesight. They can see color, but the light level they require to see well varies by species.

Nostrils—A pair of nostrils, or *nares*, is used to detect odors in the water. Sharks and sea catfish have particularly well-developed senses of smell.

Mouth—The shape of a fish's mouth is a clue to what it eats. If a fish has a large mouth, it eats large food. If it has a hard beak, it feeds on shellfish.

Teeth—Not all fish have teeth, but those that do have teeth that are adaptations to help them feed on particular prey items. Barracudas and some snappers have sharp *canine* teeth for grabbing and holding prey. Red Drum have *pharyngeal* teeth, which are located in the throat and enable them to grind shellfish. Sea catfish have *cardiform* teeth, which are bristle-like and feel like a rough patch in the front of the mouth. Striped Bass have tiny patches of *vomerine* teeth on the tongue.

Gill Cover—In most fish, the gills are protected by a hard cover, but in fish like sharks and rays, the gill openings are just slits in the skin.

Lateral Line—This sensory organ helps the fish detect movement in the water and pressure changes; this helps them avoid predators or capture prey. The lateral line consists of fluid-filled sacs with hair-like sensors, which are open to the water through a row of pores in their skin. These pores form a line along the fish's side that is very visible in some fish and almost invisible in others.

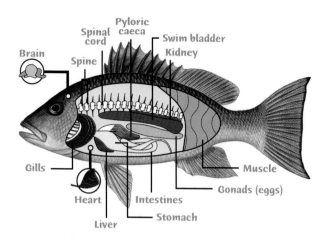

FISH NAMES

The Goliath Grouper is known as a Goliath Grouper over much of its range, but in the Florida Keys it is known as a Jewfish or a Spotted Jewfish or even the Giant Bridge Grouper. Because common names vary regionally, and can even change for different sizes of the same species, all fish are given a scientific name. Although scientific names can change through time, each species has only one recognized scientific name. The Goliath Grouper is *Epinephelus itajara* from New Orleans to Nassau.

Scientific names are made up of Greek or Latin words that often describe the species. There are two parts to a scientific name: the generic or "genus," which is capitalized (*Epinephelus*), and the specific name, which is not capitalized (*itajara*). Both are always written in italic text or underlined.

A species' genus represents a group of closely related fish. The Goliath Grouper and the Rock Hind are in the same genus, so they share the generic name *Epinephelus*. But each have different specific names, *itajara* for the Goliath Grouper, *adscensionis* for the Rock Hind.

FISH DISEASES

Like all animals, fish are susceptible to various parasites, infections and diseases, almost none of which can be passed on to humans. Ciguatera toxin is the exception. Ciguatera poisoning is caused by eating fish that have ingested a toxic dinoflagellate (a microorganism). Ciguatera toxin is very heat-resistant, so cooking affected fish does not prevent illness. Barracudas and Greater Amberjacks from warmwater reefs are two fish that are often associated with ciguatera poisoning, but it is not always present, even in these fish. It is very rare in the northern Gulf. While not often fatal, ciguatera poisoning can be debilitating and should be avoided. Check with local officials and charter captains to see if it is present where you are going to be fishing and in the species you are after. By far, most of the fish caught in the Gulf are safe to eat.

FISH CONSUMPTION ADVISORIES

Most fish are safe to eat, but pollutants in the food chain are a valid concern. Of special concern are large, predatory fish that accumulate mercury after they eat many small fish that contain mercury. All the Gulf States routinely monitor contaminant levels in fish, and each state's department of public health issues advisories on eating sport fish caught in their waters. For information about the state you're fishing in, visit that state's Department of Public Health website.

CATCH-AND-RELEASE FISHING

Selective harvest (keeping some fish to eat and releasing the rest) and total catch-and-release fishing allow anglers to enjoy the sport without harming the resource. Catch-and-release is especially important with certain species and sizes of fish, as many larger fish have been severely overharvested. Even in the ocean, fish populations are decreasing. All of the Gulf States have regulations for harvesting most of the popular sport species. Help protect the resource by following the rules.

Catch-and-release is only truly successful if the fish survives the experience. Here are some tips to help reduce the chances of post-release mortality.

- Play and land fish quickly.

- Wet your hands before touching a fish, to avoid removing its protective slime coating.

- Handle the fish gently and keep it in the water as much as possible.

- Do not hold the fish by the eyes or gills. Hold it by the lower lip or under the gill plate—and support its belly.

- If a fish is deeply hooked, cut the line so at least an inch of line hangs outside the mouth. This helps the hook lie flush when the fish takes in food.

- Circle hooks may help reduce the number of deeply hooked fish.

FISH MEASUREMENT

Fish are measured in three ways: standard length, fork length and total length. The first two are more accurate, because tails are often damaged or worn down. Total length is used when there are length regulations for keeping fish.

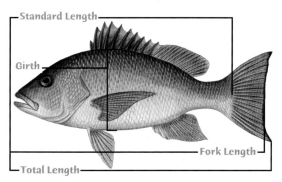

FISHING IN SALT WATER

Saltwater fishing is basically the same as freshwater fishing. The fish may be bigger, and the water more diverse, but in both environments the goal is the same: Anglers try to adopt the right equipment and techniques for the conditions at hand and the species they are seeking. There are almost limitless combinations of fishing approaches and gear, and discussing them all is well beyond the scope of this book. However, knowing a few basics will help you get started fishing in the Gulf.

Rods

Saltwater rods vary significantly depending on their purpose. When deep-bottom fishing, anglers sometimes use four-foot-long poles that are as big around as a broom handle,  whereas some anglers fishing from the beach use twelve-foot-long surf-casting whips. No rod is right for every situation, but a high-quality medium-action spinning rod that is six to eight feet long is appropriate for many coastal Gulf fishing opportunities. Graphite or a graphite-fiberglass combination will provide good feel for the bait in the water and enough backbone to land larger fish. In terms of gear, this is where to spend your money. Being able to feel the bite, then hook and land the fish is more important than how the line is being handled by the reel.

Reels

There are two basic reel designs, baitcasting reels and spinning reels. Baitcasting reels wrap the line around a central shaft and the line then unspools from the spinning shaft as the line is removed. Baitcasting reels can be large (when used for offshore trolling), or they can be small (as is the case with casting reels). In all baitcasting reels, the shaft can overrun the line being taken off, causing a tangle or "backlash." With

Baitcasting Reel

practice, this can be avoided most of the time, but is never completely eliminated.

Spinning reels wrap the line around a spool that is stationary when the line is cast. Occasionally the line coming off a spinning reel will become twisted or kinked, but this is a minor annoyance compared to the "bird's nests" common to baitcasting reels. In general, spinning reels are very forgiving and take little practice to learn to use.

Spinning Reel

Both reel varieties have advantages, but for most coastal Gulf fishing, spinning reels are the best choice. No matter which reel you choose, your reel should be large enough to hold between 200 and 300 yards of the heaviest test line you are likely to use.

Line

Most coastal Gulf fishing is done with monofilament nylon lines. These lines are easy to handle and tie. They have an added advantage too; they are flexible enough to stretch, enabling them to absorb some of the shock when a fish strikes. The new monofilaments on the block are the fluoro-carbon lines. They are extremely strong and almost invisible in the water. The downside is that they are stiff and difficult to cast. Nevertheless, fluorocarbon lines make great leaders.

In addition, there are new braided lines on the market that are much smaller in diameter than monofilaments of the same weight class. They are limp, very flexible and cast well, but they aren't flexible enough to stretch to absorb the shock of a strike, and are slick and more difficult to handle, thus making it more difficult to tie knots.

Generally speaking, good eight to twelve pound test line is adequate for most coastal Gulf fishing, if it is tipped with a leader that is 3 to 4 times stronger than the main line.

SINKERS AND FLOATS

Sinkers and floats are used to place bait where the fish are and then hold it in place. Use of a sinker or a float (or both) is necessary most of the time in saltwater fishing. While important, they can also make it more difficult to get fish to take the bait and hook them, so sinkers and floats should always be as small as possible. Nonetheless, large sinkers are sometimes necessary; deep-bottom fishing requires 8 to 10 ounces of lead sinkers. By comparison, only 2 to 4 ounces are required for  surf fishing. In all instances, using the lightest and smallest floats and sinkers possible will help you feel a fish bite and give you better control while fighting a fish.

Floats or "bobbers" are primarily used to hold bait off the bottom, but are also used as bite indicators for both bottom and surface fishing. "Popping bobbers" are also effective in attracting fish. These floats are jerked or "popped" several times after landing, and imitate the sounds made by fish feeding on the surface. Saltwater floats are not much different than freshwater floats except that they are often bigger. Saltwater floats are bigger because the baits are often larger and the water is frequently rougher; nevertheless, using the smallest float that is appropriate for the conditions will lead to the most productive fishing.

Hooks

The main difference between saltwater and freshwater hooks is their strength. Saltwater hooks are much stronger than freshwater hooks, as a large fish could potentially straighten a freshwater hook. This also applies to lures, so anglers should consider replacing the hooks on freshwater lures when fishing in the Gulf.

There are many styles of fishing hooks. Some hooks are used when fishing with particular bait, while others are used when pursuing certain gamefish species. In general, the hook's point should be exposed with the bait fitting on the hook so the space between the point and the shank is open. With increased interest in catch-and-release fishing, circle hooks are becoming very popular. These hooks hold very well once set and almost always lodge in the corner of the fish's mouth, insuring a higher survival rate for released fish. Circle hooks are not set with the typical rod jerk used with other hooks but are set with a steady pull as the line tightens. Circle hooks are the best hooks for most cut baits and work well with most live baits that are still-fished.

Standard Hook

Circle Hook

FISHING METHODS

Casting

Casting is exactly what it sounds like: throwing bait with a rod, then retrieving it. One can cast with a baitcasting rod, a spinning rod, or a fly rod. While either natural or artificial baits can be used, casting is primarily a method for artificial baits and lures, or artificial lures tipped with a natural bait. Casting is primarily a method for nearshore fishing and shallow water and has no real deepwater applications except when fishing around platforms or floating debris.

Trolling and Drifting

Trolling and drifting are two common fishing techniques that are suitable in a range of environments. Anglers in small boats often troll and drift near shore, while large, ocean-going sport trawlers troll or drift for trophies in deeper water. Still other anglers drift and troll everywhere in between.

Trolling is often used to cover large expanses of water to find fish; drifting is most often used when fish or good structure have already been located. While trolling is only one of the methods for catching many kinds of fish, it is the only practical method for catching the large pelagic (open ocean) predators like Blue Marlin and swordfish. Both artificial and natural baits are used with trolling and drifting.

23

Still-Fishing

Still-fishing is the most common and productive coastal fishing method. Particular fishing rigs may vary, but all still-fishing setups are similar: a bait is placed in the water and the fisherman waits for a bite. A wide variety of anglers  still-fish; anglers in small dinghies still-fish, as do large groups on party boats. Still-fishing is common on bridges, jetties, docks and the open surf. On a sunny beach, it can very relaxing still-fishing as you wait for a whitefish to bite, or it can be almost scary as you dangle five pounds of cut fish from a bridge at night while trying to catch a shark.

Bait is the most important part of still-fishing. Both time of day and location are important, but matching the bait to both time and location is the key to productive still-fishing. Still-fishermen typically do not move around much and are counting on the bait attracting the fish to them. Think carefully about what fish are likely to be caught where you are fishing and pick a bait likely to catch those fish, not the species that only occasionally swim by or the species you wish would come by.

BAITS
Artificial Lures

There are as many different kinds of artificial lures as there are kinds of fish, and conditions to catch them in. In general, artificial lures imitate live, often

injured, aquatic animals like fish or shrimp and are presented to entice fish into biting. Under some conditions pieces of
cut fish are added to the lure to improve the presentation or
to add taste and smell to the lure. Always keep in mind that
you are trying to imitate living creatures with your lures; this
will improve your success.

While there is no one lure that catches all fish in all conditions, the common jig comes about as close as possible. By
changing colors, tipping with different natural baits, and
varying the presentation, almost any coastal fish can be
enticed into biting a jig under some conditions.

Live Natural Baits

There are three common categories of live baits used in
coastal Gulf fishing: fish, crustaceans and marine worms.
Some of these baits must be gathered by the fishermen
themselves, but many can be
purchased in bait shops.

Baitfish used for ocean fishing
range in size from minnows
a few inches long to Bonitos
that are five pounds or larger.
Some species, such as Pinfish
and Bonitos, are considered table fare one day, and bait
the next. Others, like Ballyhoo and Needlefish, are almost
never eaten and always considered baitfish.

Shrimp, crabs and sand fleas are the most common crustaceans used as live bait in saltwater fishing. Of these, a
live shrimp is the closest thing to a universal bait as there

is. In almost any location or conditions, live shrimp will catch you something, and for some fish, such as Spotted Seatrout, a live shrimp is the best bait most of the time.

Marine worms (sand worms, blood worms and clam worms) are popular baits in some parts of the Gulf and never used in others. For the most part, small worms are considered baits for panfish, but larger worms rigged with a spinner and drifted or trolled are good seatrout and flounder baits. Jigging worms at night under the lights on a bridge or a dock can be very productive for Lookdowns and many other species.

Dead Natural Baits

There are two common ways to present dead natural baits in saltwater fishing, either whole or as cut baits. Fish and shrimp are the most popular dead whole baits, with squid being a close third. Freshly dead shrimp is a good bait for

many fish; frozen shrimp are just as good, but they are softer and harder to keep on the hook. Whole dead fish and squid are often trolled or drifted as "rigged baits." Rigged baits have multiple hooks threaded through the bait, all on a strong leader.

Cut baits are most often pieces of either fish or squid. Cut baits that consist of fish often feature the whole head or the body of a smaller fish or just a portion of a larger fish. Long strips of fish are frequently cut and used to tip lures like jigs and spoons. Squid and many other things are cut into smaller pieces and used for bait. For some fish, the meat from dead clams and oysters makes a good bait. Clams are preferable most of the time, as they are tougher and stay on the hook better. Small pieces of shelled frozen shrimp are good panfish bait throughout the Gulf.

Chum

When anglers add something to the water to attract fish, it's referred to as chumming. Chumming is a common practice in saltwater fishing. Chum can consist of a variety of items, from whole fish (live or dead) to chopped or ground fish, smashed oysters and clams, and even plain old cornmeal (which attracts baitfish). Chum can be spread on the surface to form a chum line or a slick or put in a weighted bag and lowered to the bottom. In all cases, artificial and natural baits are fished in the chum line or near the chum bag.

WHERE TO FISH

Depth

As in fresh water, depth is one of the most important factors in saltwater fishing. Different fish feed at different levels in the water column whether they are in the open Gulf or near shore. For example, some snappers school just above coral reefs while others seek cover at the  base of the coral. Finding the depth where fish are feeding is one of the challenges of catching fish. The one exception to this is shallow nearshore fishing where most species are closely associated with the bottom.

Bridges, Docks, Jetties and Fishing Piers

These can be great places to catch fish or just convenient places to go and fish. If the structure you are fishing from is in an  area that naturally attracts fish or creates a spot that fish are drawn to, then your chances of catching fish are excellent. If the structure has been built where there is little good fish habitat, then your chances of catching fish are reduced. Jetties are usually good places to fish because they were built to break the current or waves, thereby creating their own good fish habitat. Bridge and pier abutments do the same thing. As with all fishing, the time of day you're fishing and the tides will make a big difference in fishing success.

Surf

Fishing the surf is a great way to spend a day on the beach. Many surf fish often feed near the beach line and can be reached with a standard spinning rod. At other times long spinning rods are needed to cast  beyond the breakers. Learning to read the surf and understanding where the water is slightly different will help you catch more fish on the beach.

Offshore Reefs, Platforms and Wrecks

Many species of fish are attracted to man-made structures whether to hide from predators or to hunt. Some of this kind of structure is close enough to be reached safely in small boats, but much of it requires larger sport-fishing craft. Without your own craft, the best way to fish these areas is with a charter captain. They know the water and the fish and almost always put fish in the boat. Another, less expensive, way to reach such structures is to fish from a party boat. These are large boats that travel well offshore then anchor over good grouper or snapper grounds. These boats are often very productive.

The Open Ocean

The large offshore predators like marlin, tuna and large sharks are found far out in the open ocean and must be tracked down with large, powerful boats. These offshore sport craft are beyond the means of most of us but most Gulf ports have charter captains that will take you out to the offshore fishing grounds.

MARINE AND FRESHWATER FISH

Not all marine fish spend their entire life in salt water. Some enter fresh water to spawn; others spend some parts of the year feeding in fresh water. Similarly, some freshwater fish routinely enter salt water (mostly brackish water), with some even venturing out to the open seas. Some of the species that move back and forth between salt and fresh water are listed below.

Freshwater Fish That Enter Salt Water or Brackish Water

These are a few freshwater fish from the Gulf States that are routinely found in brackish or salt water.

Largemouth Bass	Bowfin	White Catfish
Freshwater Drum	Chain Pickerel	Spotted Sunfish
Yellow Bass	Common Carp	Black Crappie
Alligator Gar	Grass Pickerel	Warmouth
Black Bullhead	Channel Catfish	White Crappie
Shortnose Gar	Brook Silverside	
Yellow Bullhead	Flathead Catfish	
Sheepshead Minnow	Redear Sunfish	

Marine Fish That Enter Fresh Water or Brackish Water

These are a few marine fish from the Gulf States that are routinely found in fresh water.

Striped Bass	Gray Snapper
Sand Seatrout	Jack Crevalle
Hardhead Catfish	Spot
Spotted Seatrout	Ladyfish
Atlantic Croaker	Atlantic Stingray
Bull Shark	Striped Mullet
Red Drum	Tarpon
Sheepshead	Pinfish
Southern Flounder	Southern Puffer

HOW TO USE THIS BOOK

This book is organized alphabetically, first by family then by species.

To Find Your Fish:

1. If you know the family, look it up in the Table of Contents and go to that section.

2. If you don't know the family, look through the Table of Contents to match the silhouette of your fish, and go to that section.

3. Page through the images until you find a match.

4. Read the description to be sure the characteristics match.

The Table of Contents (pg. 3) lists all the families and individual species. The Index (pg. 193) lists fish by their common and/or popular names.

Helpful Notes:

- Fish frequently change colors, so illustrations may not match your fish precisely

- Males are more brightly colored during the spawning season

- Habitat can affect color; a fish from muddy water may have less color than a fish from clear water

- All fish lose some color when removed from the water

These pages explain how the information is presented for each fish.

SAMPLE FISH ILLUSTRATION

Description: brief summary of physical characteristics to help you identify the fish, such as coloration and markings, body shape, fin size and placement

FISHING TIPS

Methods: the common methods used to catch this fish, such as casting, trolling, drifting or still-fishing

Bait: the common baits used to catch this fish such as fish, shrimp, squid or cut baits

Where: the places you are most likely to catch this fish

Tips: tips on how to catch more of this species

COMMON NAME
Scientific Name

Other Names: the common terms or nicknames you may hear to describe the fish

Habitat: environment where the fish is likely found (such as on reefs or near wrecks, in coastal estuaries or bays)

Food: what the fish commonly feeds on

Reproduction: a short description of the reproductive habits of the fish

Gulf Distribution: the parts of the Gulf of Mexico where the species is likely to be found

Average Size: the average length or weight of the species when caught in the Gulf of Mexico

World Record: the world record for the fish as published by the International Game Fish Association

Table Quality: note on the edibility and preparation of this fish for the table

Notes: Interesting natural history information. This can include unique behaviors, remarkable features, sporting quality, or details on migrations, seasonal patterns or population trends.

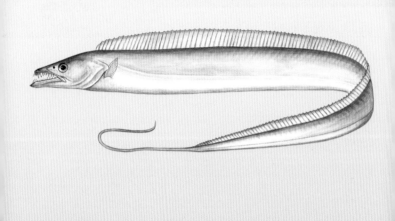

Description: bright, silver, long strap-shaped body; no scales; large head, mouth and eyes; mouth full of large, sharp teeth; long dorsal fin extending from head to tail; no pelvic fin; long, thin tail

FISHING

Methods: casting, drifting and still-fishing

Bait: live bait and lures, infrequently caught on still-fished cut baits

Where: bridges, piers and breakwaters and inland bays during warm weather; slightly offshore during colder weather

Tip: a small silver spoon with a strip of cut fish works well for cutlassfish

ATLANTIC CUTLASSFISH
Trichiurus lepturus

Other Names: ribbonfish, silver eel, silverfish, dragonfish

Habitat: bays, cuts and harbors out to shallow open water

Food: small fish and shrimp

Reproduction: little is known of the life cycle of the cutlassfish

Gulf Distribution: the entire Gulf, but especially abundant from Louisiana through Texas

Average Size: 2 to 4 feet

World Record: 8 pounds, 1 ounce, Brazil, 1997

Table Quality: good flavor, but oily and bony; rarely eaten in this country

Notes: Atlantic Cutlassfish are voracious feeders that are often caught by anglers on piers and jetties using live bait or small lures. Cutlassfish often attack hooked fish as anglers reel them in. They are not strong fighters or hardy out of water and die soon after being landed. Their teeth are sharp and can inflict a painful wound, but Cutlassfish are not venomous as often reported. They are considered a nuisance in most of the Gulf, but in Louisiana and Texas they are a preferred trolling bait for mackerel. Their oily flesh makes good cut bait. Though not often eaten in this country, they support commercial fisheries in other parts of the world.

Description: long, torpedo-shaped body with a pointed head; dark gray-green back and silver-gray sides; dark blotches on lower sides; some fish have dark diagonal bands on upper sides; large, sharp teeth

FISHING

> **Methods:** casting lures and flies, trolling, drifting and still-fishing
>
> **Bait:** live fish and lures
>
> **Where:** small fish are found inshore near grassy flats and mangrove edges; larger fish are found offshore near platforms, wrecks and reefs
>
> **Tips:** barracuda can be lure-shy; fishing a whole baitfish with a small spinner works well at these times

GREAT BARRACUDA

Sphyraena barracuda

Other Names: cuda, sea or giant sea pike, silver pike

Habitat: near shore around grassy flats and out to deep water with structure in the southern Gulf; mostly deep water in the northern Gulf

Food: almost exclusively fish

Reproduction: barracudas mature at 2 to 3 years old and spawn from late spring throughout the summer

Gulf Distribution: entire Gulf

Average Size: inshore—1 to 5 pounds, offshore—15 to 30 pounds

World Record: 85 pounds; Kiribati, 1992

Table Quality: small fish have excellent flavor; large fish from warm water often harbor the toxin ciguatera and should be avoided

Notes: Barracudas are fast, aggressive fish that are renowned for striking flashy moving objects in the water, whether it's a fish, a lure or the occasional wedding ring or watch. Despite this (and their propensity to stalk divers) they are not considered a particularly dangerous fish. Small 'cudas caught near shore on light spinning tackle or a fly rod make strong runs and spectacular jumps. Offshore, barracudas are common near wrecks, reefs and oil platforms and are hard fighters when caught on suitable tackle. Though barracudas are normally aggressive biters, they occasionally reject all lures and can only be enticed with live bait.

37

Description: torpedo-shaped body; sword extending from snout (not present in young fish); dark blue back fading to silver sides; light vertical bars on upper sides (absent in older fish); pointed dorsal fin not as deep as body; anal fin almost as deep as dorsal fin; lateral line branches on rear half of fish

FISHING

Methods: trolling, drifting

Bait: small fish, squid, lures and flies

Where: offshore, near baitfish schools and floating vegetation

Tips: when strikes are slow, baiting some rods with large squid often helps

BLUE MARLIN
Makaira nigricans

Other Names: Atlantic blue marlin, blue swordfish

Habitat: open ocean worldwide

Food: fish, squid and cuttlefish

Reproduction: little is known about blue marlin spawning; females mature at about 100 pounds; gravid (egg-bearing) females are caught from late summer to early fall in the Gulf

Gulf Distribution: open seas of the entire Gulf during warm weather; the southern Gulf in winter

Average Size: 12 to 14 feet, 150 to 450 pounds

World Record: 1,402 pounds, 2 ounces, Vitoria, Brazil, 1992

Table Quality: excellent, but not often eaten by sportfishermen; often marketed as swordfish

Notes: The Blue Marlin's large size and spectacular leaps when hooked make it one of the world's premier sport fish. The largest fish are always females; the male normally reaching only a third of the female's weight. The Blue Marlin from the Pacific is the same species as the Atlantic fish, but Pacific marlins are slightly smaller on average. The largest fish range the open ocean well beyond a day's fishing trip, but 500-pounders are not uncommon in the northern Gulf and much larger fish are present in the southern Gulf.

Description: long, thin compressed body; snout with long spear; dark blue back fading to silver sides (occasionally bronze) with light pale vertical bars; large, deep dorsal fin (150% body depth); long pelvic fins almost reach anal fin

FISHING

Methods: trolling, kite fishing and drifting

Bait: live and rigged fish, squid and lures

Where: near and offshore open ocean

Tips: in the southern Gulf sailfish may come relatively close to shore, anglers for other fish should keep an eye open for the opportunity

SAILFISH
Istiophorus platypterus

Other Names: blue sailfish, Atlantic sailfish, spindlebeak, bayonetfish

Habitat: open seas near to offshore, often over reefs or breaks

Food: fish, squid, cuttlefish and octopus

Reproduction: spawns during summer months in nearshore waters; several males associate with a single female that lays 800,000 to 1,500,000 eggs

Gulf Distribution: Gulf-wide in warm weather; common year around in the southern Gulf, particularly in the Florida Straits and southern Mexico

Average Size: 4 to 7 feet, 20 to 40 pounds

World Record: 141 pounds, 1 ounce, Angola, 1994

Table Quality: excellent baked or smoked, but not often eaten by sportfishermen; similar to swordfish in flavor

Notes: Sailfish are one of the most highly prized sport fish in the Gulf of Mexico. The Florida Straits are the premier sailfish waters in the Gulf, but a good number of fish are caught throughout the northern Gulf in warm weather. Unlike Blue Marlin, Sailfish are often found in open water relatively close to shore. They also differ from Blue Marlin in that Sailfish in the Pacific are larger than those in the Atlantic; the opposite is true for Blue Marlin. Sailfish are frequently found cruising reefs and current breaks. Like other marine fish, their numbers are dwindling and every effort should be made to release hooked fish unharmed.

41

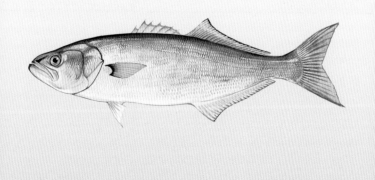

Description: blue-green back and upper sides fading to silver on lower sides and belly; large mouth with very sharp teeth; forked tail; dorsal fin is divided, rear portion is higher and twice as long as front portion; anal fin same shape and almost as long as rear dorsal fin; dark spot at base of pectoral fins

FISHING

Methods: casting, trolling, drifting and still-fishing

Bait: live fish and shrimp, cut baits and lures

Where: surf and piers, grassy flats to nearshore open water

Tips: a Johnson spoon (hook sharpened) tipped with cut fish is good for larger Bluefish in the surf

BLUEFISH
Pomatomus saltatrix

Other Names: blue or Hatteras blue, rock salmon, snapper, snap mackerel, skipjack, chopper, marine piranha

Habitat: surf and bays out to open water with some structure or vegetation

Food: varied diet; fish, shrimp, crabs and lobsters

Reproduction: Bluefish reportedly spawn both offshore in open water and in nearshore estuaries

Gulf Distribution: common in the eastern Gulf; less common from Louisiana through Texas

Average Size: 1 to 2 pounds

World Record: 31 pounds, 12 ounces, Hatteras, North Carolina, 1972

Table Quality: fair, but only when eaten within a day; flesh is oily and best smoked or broiled

Notes: Bluefish are a common catch from fishing piers and in the surf. In some parts of the Gulf, Bluefish are considered a nuisance, particularly when small. In other parts of the Gulf, and on the East Coast, large Bluefish are considered a great sport fish. They are voracious feeders and strong fighters. They deserve their nickname of "chopper," as they use their sharp teeth to cut leaders and bite unwary fishermen after being landed. On occasion, Bluefish have even been known to take a bite out of a swimmer.

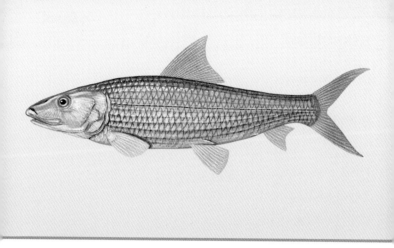

Description: elongated, stout body with pointed head and
black-tipped snout; underslung mouth; bright silver sides,
back greenish blue; young fish with dark bands on back; no
elongated dorsal fin rays

FISHING

Methods: casting lures and flies, still-fishing

Bait: lures, flies, shrimp, small pieces of clam

Where: shallow mud and grass flats

Tips: still-fish channels near deep flats with clams, watch
for mud boils when sight-fishing; a rising tide seems best

BONEFISH
Albula vulpes

Other Names: white fox, ghost fish or silver ghost, white or silver streak

Habitat: warm, shallow coastal water and deeper flats down to about 30 feet; often found in mangrove and coral bays with a soft bottom

Food: crabs, clams, sea urchins and small fish

Reproduction: spawns from late spring through early summer; young look like tiny eels until about $2\frac{1}{2}$ inches long, then shrink and morph into fish-like fry

Gulf Distribution: southern Florida; less common to rare in northern and western Gulf

Average Size: 2 to 5 pounds

World Record: 19 pounds, Zululand, South Africa

Table Quality: Not often eaten in this country

Notes: Bonefish are a premier sport fish in the warm Gulf waters of Southern Florida and the Yucatan. They are not common in the northern Gulf but are sometimes caught in the surf from Mississippi to Texas. Bonefish are frequently "hunted" from a flats boat that is poled through the shallows. When feeding fish are sighted, flies or lures are cast toward the fish. Large schools of Bonefish sometimes gather over deep flats but the larger fish, commonly up to 10 pounds, are mostly solitary feeders. Bonefish are hard strikers and tremendous fighters on light tackle but are rarely kept for the table.

45

Description: long, narrow, dark brown body fading to tan on lower sides; darker stripe on sides from eye to tail; stripe fades in larger fish and is white above and black below in young fish; narrow, flattened head with protruding lower lip; all fins are dark brown; long, soft dorsal fin preceded by 8 to 10 spines; dorsal fin longer than anal fin

FISHING

Methods: casting, trolling, drifting and still-fishing

Bait: live fish, squid, crabs and lures

Where: shallow open ocean around buoys, platforms, wrecks and anchored boats; frequently caught from fishing piers or bridges

Tips: inshore buoys and channel markers often attract Cobia and should be checked out

COBIA

Rachycentron canadum

Other Names: ling, cabio, lemonfish, crabeater, sergeantfish, black salmon or kingfish

Habitat: shallow open ocean around platforms, buoys and wrecks; young fish frequent inshore waters and bays

Food: mostly crabs and shrimp, but some fish, squid and eels

Reproduction: Cobia mature at 2 to 3 years and spawn just offshore or in deeper nearshore waters throughout the summer

Gulf Distribution: the entire Gulf during warm weather; migrates to deeper water and the southern Gulf in winter

Average Size: 10 to 40 pounds

World Record: 135 pounds, 9 ounces, Australia, 1985

Table Quality: this highly prized food fish has a unique, mild flavor and is good however it is prepared

Notes: The Cobia is a great coastal sport fish for anglers that have access to a small boat. They frequent the open water close to shore and are attracted to floating structure and wrecks, so they are relatively easy to locate, often near the surface. Cobia are normally strong fighters but on occasion they are landed with little effort then come to life in the boat, quickly smashing things up. Cobia only loosely associate in schools and are often found as lone fish, so they are not as susceptible to commercial harvest as some other species. Cobia is one of the premier food fish of the Gulf States, but it is only available to fishermen, as it not found often in stores.

Description: deep body with arched back; young fish silver-gray with 4 or 5 wide vertical bars; older fish lack bars and are dark silver with a brassy sheen; fins dark silver to black; head blunt with low horizontal mouth and many chin barbels

FISHING

> **Methods:** still-fishing, drifting and casting
>
> **Bait:** crabs, clams, squid and cut fish
>
> **Where:** docks, piers, bridges; surf and channels for larger fish
>
> **Tips:** fish the mouth of small bays and estuaries on the falling tide for eating-sized Black Drum

BLACK DRUM

Pogonias cromis

Other Names: common, striped or sea drum

Habitat: in bays and channels near shore; surf off open ocean

Food: crabs, clams, mussels, oysters, shrimp and a few fish

Reproduction: spawning schools gather in open water at the mouth of rivers and channels in late spring; large females may lay 6 million eggs

Gulf Distribution: entire Gulf, particularly abundant in western Louisiana and Texas

Average Size: 2 to 30 pounds

World Record: 113 pounds, 1 ounce, Bahamas, 2002

Table Quality: small fish are very good; large fish are coarse and best ground up for fish cakes or used in stews

Notes: Black Drum are a very common fish in nearshore waters throughout the Gulf. They feed near the bottom, using the large, flat teeth in their throats to grind up shellfish. Young fish are often mistaken for sheepsheads, but lack the sheepshead's prominent front teeth. Larger drum lack stripes and prefer deep channels or offshore water. Black drum are not hard strikers; they bite with a slow tug that is perfect for setting circle hooks. Once hooked, Black drum make steady, strong, but not frantic, runs.

Description: elongated dark copper or bronze body; fins dark coppery brown; dark spot at base of tail above lateral line (occasionally multiple spots); snout protrudes beyond lower lip; no barbels on chin

FISHING

Methods: casting, drifting and still-fishing

Bait: live shrimp, fish, crabs, or bloodworms, flies, cut bait and lures

Where: piers, jetties and surf, shell bars and rocky shorelines, grassy or muddy flats

Tips: a white jig tipped with a shrimp is a good combination for use over oyster beds

RED DRUM
Sciaenops ocellatus

Other Names: channel, spot-tail or red bass, school or puppy drum, red or redfish, bull drum

Habitat: widespread in coastal bays, estuaries and the surf of the open ocean; "bull redfish" are found just outside of deeper channels; young fish frequent shallow flats

Food: crabs, shrimp, sand dollars and fish

Reproduction: spawning takes place at dusk in coastal channels in late fall and winter

Gulf Distribution: common throughout the entire Gulf

Average Size: 3 to 10 pounds; 15- to 20-pounders are not uncommon

World Record: 94 pounds, 2 ounces, Avon, North Carolina, 1984

Table Quality: fish up to about 10 pounds are excellent; bigger fish are coarse, stringy and only suitable for fish patties

Notes: The Red Drum is an important sport fish throughout the Gulf of Mexico but reaches peak importance from Louisiana through the large Texas bays. The chefs from New Orleans have made blackened redfish famous. Red Drum are bottom-feeders that often feed with their heads down and tails sticking up. This posture aids in rooting shellfish and small fish out of the sediments. Large "bull drum" (always females) seek deeper water and are often found just outside of deep channels. Redfish will readily strike a large variety of artificial lures, but are most often fished with live shrimp or minnows.

51

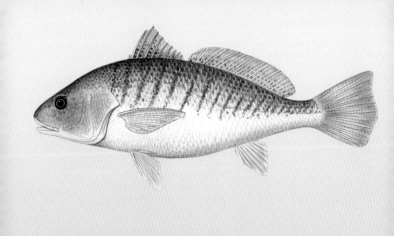

Description: deep body with arched back; silver-gray back fading to grayish white sides (spawning fish are yellow-bronze); the vertical lines on upper sides are formed by a dark spot at the base of each scale; paired fins yellow to light brown; spots on base of rear dorsal fin; small barbels on lower jaw

FISHING

Methods: still-fishing

Bait: sand fleas, cut fish, shrimp or squid

Where: piers, docks, jetties and surf over a soft bottom

Tips: fish small pieces of clam over a bar on an incoming tide

ATLANTIC CROAKER

Micropogonias undulatus

Other Names: croaker, grunt fish, golden croaker, hardhead, kingbilly

Habitat: inshore waters over a soft bottom of mud, mixed shells and sand

Food: clams, shrimp and small fish

Reproduction: spawns from early fall through winter in the open sea at channel mouths; fry quickly migrate to inland shallows

Gulf Distribution: common throughout the northern Gulf

Average Size: $\frac{1}{2}$ to 1 pound

World Record: 8 pounds, 11 ounces, Chesapeake Bay, Virginia, 2007

Table Quality: a great panfish with firm, white flesh; bread and fry whole

Notes: Atlantic croakers are small bottom-feeding fish that prefer the cooler portions of the Gulf. In the Gulf they range from less than a pound to over 2 pounds, but not nearly as large as the giants from Chesapeake Bay that run 4 to 5 pounds. During the fall spawning period, Atlantic croakers turn a bronzy gold and gather just outside passes and channels. The name croaker comes from the grunting noise made when they are handled. Croakers are easily caught when still-fishing the bottom with light tackle tipped with small pieces of peeled shrimp.

53

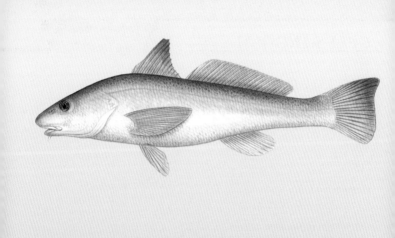

Description: Both—narrow body; mouth under head; single barbel under chin; tail is asymmetrical; upper tail lobe is shorter and slightly pointed; Gulf—dark gray back and silver sides; black tip on tail; Southern—brownish gray with dark bands on the sides that fade in larger fish; no black tip on tail

FISHING

Methods: casting and still-fishing

Bait: sand fleas, shrimp, crabs, cut bait, bloodworms, flies and small lures

Where: primarily in the surf over sand, occasionally in open bays with a sandy bottom

Tips: kingfish are often in the shallow water just at the surf line

Sciaenidae

GULF KINGFISH
Menticirrhus littoralis

SOUTHERN KINGFISH *Menticirrhus americanus*

Other Names: whiting or Gulf whiting, surf cod, sea mullet

Habitat: primarily surf waters over sand; Southern Kingfish enter bays more frequently

Food: small crustaceans, shrimp and fish

Reproduction: spawning takes place just offshore in late spring or early summer

Gulf Distribution: common in the northern Gulf; less common in the far southern Gulf

Average Size: less than a pound

World Record: Gulf Kingfish—3 pounds, Salvo, North Carolina, 1999; Southern Kingfish—2 pounds, 13 ounces, Virginia Beach, Virginia, 2002

Table Quality: very good when eaten fresh; best dipped in a good beer batter and fried

Notes: There are two kingfish species common in the Gulf, the Southern and Gulf. They have the same body characteristics but are different colors. The Gulf Kingfish is silver-gray; the Southern Kingfish has a brownish cast. Both are primarily surf fish that prefer moving water with a sand bottom. Southern Kingfish are more likely to enter inland bays than Gulf Kingfish and the Southern Kingfish is sometimes very abundant in shallow estuaries. They both are excellent table fare if put on ice as soon as caught and eaten fresh.

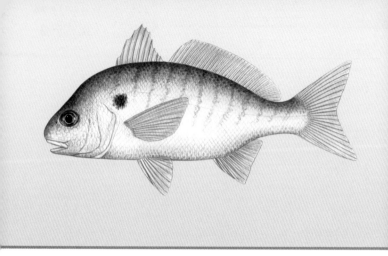

Description: deep, stout silver-gray body with bronze over-tones; 12 to 15 angled bronze bars from back to about the lateral line; a dark spot the size of the eye behind gills and just above base of pectoral fin; slightly forked tail

FISHING

Methods: still-fishing

Bait: cut fish, shrimp and squid

Where: docks, piers and jetties

Tips: a small white jig tipped with a squid tentacle works well when a school is located

SPOT
Leiostomus xanthurus

Other Names: Norfolk spot, spotted or flat croaker, spotfish, Lafayette

Habitat: shallow bays and estuaries, beaches outside of heavy surf line

Food: small crustaceans, sand worms, shrimp and fish

Reproduction: spawns in open water just offshore during the late fall in the northern Gulf and early spring in the southern Gulf

Gulf Distribution: entire Gulf

Average Size: 6 to 10 inches, under a pound

World Record: 1 pound, 6 ounces, Virginia Beach, Virginia, 2004

Table Quality: excellent flavored panfish; deep fry whole

Notes: The Spot is a small fish that is found in large schools in the shallow waters of the Gulf and Atlantic coasts. On the East Coast they are considered a prime panfish, but they are not highly prized in most of the Gulf. The Spot congregates in large schools and is targeted by commercial fishermen in the East, where millions of pounds are harvested each year. Like other croakers, the Spot makes a grunting noise when handled. When schools of Spots are located, fishermen can catch large numbers using small pieces of cut bait. Spots are excellent when pan-fried and yield more meat than the popular freshwater Bluegill.

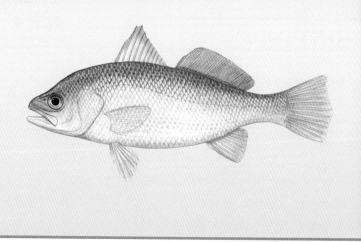

Description: shiny silver body; very light stripes along sides that are most visible above lateral line; large reddish-yellow eye; yellow translucent tail, anal and pelvic fins

FISHING

Methods: casting, still-fishing

Bait: small pieces of fish, shrimp or squid

Where: deep water near docks, jetties, bridges and very salty coastal streams

Tips: live Silver Perch are good Bluefish and Striped Bass bait

SILVER PERCH

Bairdiella chrysoura

Other Names: yellowtail, silver trout, silverfish, sugar trout

Habitat: moderately deep water in saltier bays, often near grass flats or coastal streams

Food: small crustaceans and fish

Reproduction: spawning takes place in the spring in shallow coastal waters near inlets

Gulf Distribution: entire Gulf; less common in southern waters

Average Size: 6 inches, less than 1 pound

World Record: none

Table Quality: small but with good flavor, roll in cornmeal and fry whole

Notes: This small, silver fish is considered a complete nuisance by most anglers. They are persistent bait robbers but are not often big enough to take home. The larger ones are very tasty when scaled and fried whole like other panfish. At times, schools of Silver Perch will chase small baitfish to the surface, fooling anglers into thinking that larger game fish are in the area. Silver Perch are reasonably hardy and make good live bait. They remain shiny after death, so they also make good dead float baits for drifting and still-fishing.

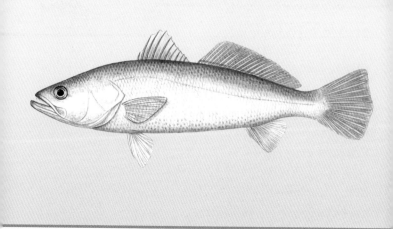

Description: long, slender body; dark yellow-green back occasionally with a pinkish cast; dark blotches on upper back; pale silver sides; large eye and mouth; sharp canine teeth on upper lip; usually 10 or 11 rays in anal fin

FISHING

Methods: casting, drifting and still-fishing

Bait: shrimp, squid, minnows, cut bait and lures

Where: deeper bays, channels

Tips: drift live shrimp near the bottom in channels in deep bays; use a graphite rod to detect soft bites

SAND SEATROUT

Cynoscion arenarius

Sciaenidae

Other Names: white or sand trout, white or sand weakfish

Habitat: deep bays, channels and shallow open areas of the Gulf, most often over a sand or shell bottom

Food: shrimp, squid, octopus and fish

Reproduction: spawns in open Gulf throughout the warm months

Gulf Distribution: entire Gulf

Average Size: 12 to 15 inches, $1^1/_2$ to 2 pounds

World Record: 6 pounds, 2 ounces, Dauphin Island, Alabama, 1997

Table Quality: good flavor, but meat can be soft

Notes: Seatrout are popular sport fish throughout the Gulf. Sand Seatrout are similar in appearance to the larger Spotted Seatrout but lack the distinctive spots on the body and tail. Sand Seatrout prefer deeper water than Spotted Seatrout and are frequently caught in the open Gulf as well as in deep channels and bays and only rarely over shallow bars or grass flats. Like the other seatrout species, the flesh is fragile and can become a little soft if not handled with care. Putting your fish on ice as soon as they are landed helps keep the meat firm.

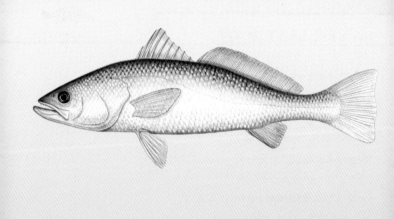

Description: long, slender body; light yellow-green back (paler than Sand Seatrout); silver-white sides; large mouth and eye; sharp canine teeth on upper lip; 8 or 9 soft rays in anal fin

FISHING

Methods: casting, drifting and still-fishing

Bait: fish, shrimp, squid, cut baits and lures

Where: shallow, open Gulf in summer; deeper bays and channels in winter

Tips: Silver Seatrout are often concentrated in deep inland channels in winter and respond well to white jigs tipped with shrimp

SILVER SEATROUT
Cynoscion nothus

Sciaenidae

Other Names: silver trout, silver weakfish

Habitat: shallow open Gulf and deep bays and channels from 20 to 70 feet deep

Food: shrimp, squid, octopus and fish

Reproduction: little is known of this seatrout's life history but it is thought to spawn offshore in the fall

Gulf Distribution: present in entire Gulf

Average Size: 6 to 10 inches, under 1 pound

World Record: 1 pound, 4 ounces, Aransas Pass, Texas, 2006

Table Quality: small panfish with soft flesh, but they have very good flavor

Notes: The Silver Seatrout is the smallest of the three common seatrout species found in the Gulf of Mexico. They are also the seatrout species that prefers the deepest water and the one most often caught in the open Gulf. Seatrout are called weakfish on the East Coast because of their weak or soft flesh and Silver Seatrout has the weakest or softest flesh of all seatrout species. Despite the Silver Seatrout's small size and soft flesh, they make a fine panfish if they are put on ice when landed, then scaled and fried whole.

Description: long, slender body; dark gray-green back with
a blue cast; dark back fades to silver sides; dark spots on
upper body, dorsal and tail fin; large mouth and eye; orange
inside of mouth; sharp canine teeth on upper lip

FISHING

Methods: casting, drifting and still-fishing

Bait: live shrimp and baitfish, cut baits and lures

Where: shallow grass and shell flats

Tips: brightly colored, soft-bodied lures that are fished
very slowly are effective

SPOTTED SEATROUT

Sciaenidae

Cynoscion nebulosus

Other Names: spotted weakfish, squeteague, speck, speckled, gator, winter, or salmon trout

Habitat: grass and shell flats in shallow protected bays; surf and deeper water in cool weather

Food: fish, shrimp and crabs

Reproduction: spawns in deep bays and estuaries throughout the spring, summer and fall

Gulf Distribution: the entire Gulf

Average Size: 12 to 18 inches, 2 to 5 pounds

World Record: 17 pounds, 7 ounces, Ft. Pierce, Florida, 1995

Table Quality: excellent table fare with fine texture and great flavor

Notes: The Spotted Seatrout is one of the most popular food, sport and commercial fish of the coastal Gulf States. Spotted Seatrout are shallow-water bottom-feeding fish. On occasion, Spotted Seatrout can be found almost anywhere in shallow Gulf waters, but they are most frequently caught on grass or shell flats. Shrimp are the primary food of smaller trout; larger trout prefer small fish. Plastic-tailed jigs, silver spoons and casting plugs are popular lures for Spotted Seatrout. Fly fishermen prefer poppers for shallow-feeding fish and pink or red bucktails for fish in deep water. Like other seatrout species, Spotted Seatrout don't keep well and should be handled with care after landing.

Description: body is deep at the head tapering to narrow restriction at tail; males have steep, blunt forehead; metallic blue-green back; sides are yellow-gold, metallic green to yellow-green; females are often metallic blue on sides; dorsal fin runs from head to tail; deeply forked tail with pointed lobes

FISHING

Methods: trolling, drifting and casting

Bait: small fish, squid, flies and lures

Where: open Gulf near floating vegetation

Tips: the new soft-bodied squid lures are very productive at dawn and dusk

DOLPHIN
Coryphaena hippurus

Other Names: dorado, mahi-mahi, dolphinfish, goldmackerel

Habitat: surface water of open Gulf often near floating vegetation and platforms; occasionally deep nearshore waters

Food: fish, squid, shrimp and sea turtles

Reproduction: spawns in the open sea from November through July, depending on latitude

Gulf Distribution: entire Gulf

Average Size: 5 to 15 pounds

World Record: 87 pounds, Costa Rica, 1976

Table Quality: excellent table fare; basting with a lime-garlic butter while grilling is a great way to prepare Dolphin

Notes: The Dolphin is a premier offshore game fish found in the Gulf of Mexico. It is beautiful, abundant, a spectacular fighter and excellent on the table. In order to prevent confusion with the warm-blooded mammal, Dolphin is marketed commercially as mahi-mahi or dolphinfish. Dolphins are a fast-growing fish that seldom live past 3 or 4 years. They are often found in large schools cruising near the surface while feeding on flying fish and squid. Dolphins are attracted to floating objects and are frequently found under platforms or mats of vegetation.

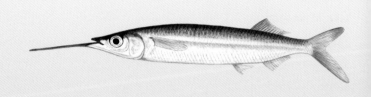

Description: long, narrow body; silver-green back; sides
have a blue-gold sheen with a silver stripe; long lower jaw
protrudes into a beak; dorsal fin, lower jaw and the tip of
the tail's upper lobe are all orange; lower lobe of tail longer
than upper lobe

FISHING

Methods: cast netting, seines and still-fishing

Bait: ground chum

Where: lighted piers and bridges

Tips: suspending light sticks just under the surface will
often concentrate halfbeaks if they are nearby

BALLYHOO
Hemirhamphus

Other Names: balao, halfbeak, green halfbeak

Habitat: over shoals and reefs in open coastal waters

Food: small fish and shrimp

Reproduction: little is known of their natural history, but they are thought to spawn over reefs and rock ledges

Gulf Distribution: entire Gulf

Average Size: 10 to 15 inches

World Record: none

Table Quality: seldom eaten in the US

Notes: There are several species of halfbeaks found in the Gulf. The Balao and Ballyhoo are two of the largest and most common. The halfbeaks are important baitfish for offshore trolling. Ballyhoos travel in large schools and are often concentrated over shoals and reefs. They are primarily netted but can be caught with hook and line using small cut baits drifted near the surface. They are also readily available as frozen bait. Ballyhoos are not often eaten in this country but are a prized table fish in the Caribbean and reportedly excellent when grilled.

Description: deep, stout body; black mantle over head and back; sides white with dark bands; pectoral fin gray, all other fins black; each scale on upper body has a dark spot at base; mouth small with thick lips

FISHING

Methods: drifting and still-fishing

Bait: shrimp, small crabs and cut bait

Where: docks, rocky piers, jetties, reefs and surf

Tips: use clam meat as bait; fish in the surf with a heavy egg sinker that rolls around disturbing the sand a little

BLACK MARGATE

Anisotremus surinamensis

Other Names: black, surf or rock bream, black grunt

Habitat: shallow coastal waters with a rock or shell bottom, rocky surf to deeper reefs just off shore

Food: shrimp, clams and small fish

Reproduction: spawns over rocky shoals throughout the warm months

Gulf Distribution: entire Gulf

Average Size: 2 to 5 pounds

World Record: 12 pounds, 12 ounces, Ft. Pierce Inlet, Florida, 1994

Table Quality: good to excellent; bake stuffed or grilled

Notes: The Black Margate is a deep-bodied fish that is often confused with the Sheepshead. They both are common around rocky structure, but on close examination they are easy to differentiate. Margates have rounded tail lobes and black fins; Sheepsheads have pointed tail lobes and light fins. Black Margates do not have the Sheepshead's sharp front teeth, so they are not as hard to hook as Sheepsheads. Margates are strong fighters and very sporting when caught on light tackle. Small clams are the best bait but shrimp and cut bait also work well.

Description: laterally compressed bluish-gray body; many
bronze markings on sides; head with bronze bars; small eye
and mouth; thin lips

FISHING

Methods: still-fishing and drifting

Bait: shrimp and cut baits

Where: shallow water along docks, jetties, channel banks
and over grass flats

Tips: fish bloodworms or squid tentacles on the bottom
with a two-hook rig in muddy channels

PIGFISH
Orthopristis chrysoptera

Other Names: hogfish, piggy, piggy perch, grunt or orange spotted grunt

Habitat: shallow coastal waters often over a mud bottom; winters just offshore

Food: shrimp, clams and small fish

Reproduction: spawns offshore just before migrating inshore for the warm months

Gulf Distribution: the entire Gulf

Average Size: 4 to 8 inches

World Record: none

Table Quality: good panfish, but seldom eaten in the Gulf; on the East Coast, they are highly prized and marketed commercially

Notes: The Pigfish is a small, very common fish of the shallow coastal Gulf waters. Pigfish are schooling, nocturnal fish that frequent muddy, shallow bays. They are not often eaten but are very popular for bait. The grunting sound Pigfish make when used for bait and stressed is thought to attract larger predatory fish. Pigfish are often confused with Pinfish but have a much smaller eye and mouth and lack the sharp spines in the dorsal fin. A good place to catch Pigfish is along the banks of channels and salty coastal streams.

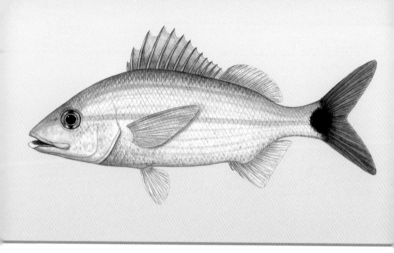

Description: deep silver-white body; yellow-brown stripe running from snout to a dark spot at base of tail; large mouth and eye; deeply forked tail

FISHING

> **Methods:** still-fishing
>
> **Bait:** small pieces of shrimp, squid or fish
>
> **Where:** docks, jetties and piers
>
> **Tips:** fish at night with small pieces of clam

TOMTATE
Haemulidae

Haemulon aurolineatum

Other Names: brown grunt, tommy grunt

Habitat: shallow inshore waters; nearshore reefs and rock ledges

Food: worms, clams, shrimp, snails and crabs

Reproduction: spawns over reefs in early spring

Gulf Distribution: entire Gulf

Average Size: 4 to 8 inches

World Record: none

Table Quality: too small to eat, but popular for bait

Notes: Tomtates are one of the small bait robbers that live around docks and jetties. Mostly nocturnal, they gather in large schools feeding on small food items near the bottom. In the evening, these large schools often migrate from the rocky reefs to grass flats. Tomtates withstand cooler temperatures better than many other Gulf fish and in winter they can still be found in very shallow water. In winter, Tomtates are often the easiest baitfish to catch in large numbers. When on a reef, they are a common food for snappers and groupers.

Description: deep body with a dark green back and silver sides; has a dark spot on the upper back edge of gill and occasionally one on the shoulder; deep rounded belly; deeply forked tail

FISHING

Methods: hoop or cast nets, bait rings, still-fishing, non-baited gold hooks

Bait: ground fish chum

Where: grassy flats; shallow water near structure

Tips: chum with a mixture of dried and canned cat food

SCALED SARDINE
Harengula jaguana

Other Names: pilchard, whitebait, silverbait

Habitat: inshore grassy flats and shallow water near bridges and jetties; offshore near wrecks and navigation markers

Food: floating plankton

Reproduction: spawns in open water throughout the warmer months

Gulf Distribution: entire Gulf

Average Size: 4 to 6 inches

World Record: none

Table Quality: not often eaten in US, but popular in the Caribbean and the West Indies

Notes: The Scaled Sardine is one of several species that are known as pilchards or whitebait. They are very abundant in the Gulf and prized in most areas as bait. They can be caught with non-baited gold hooks but are more frequently concentrated with chum, then netted or caught with a specialized device called a pilchard or ring rig. Sardines are not often eaten fresh in this country but are very popular for grilling in Spain. In the Caribbean they are often cooked with other small fish known collectively as grilled "whitebait."

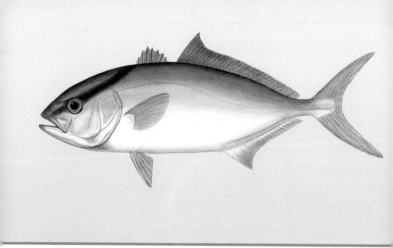

Description: a heavy body that is shallower than in other jacks; dark brown to bluish brown above, tan below; faint bronze-yellow stripe on side; dark olive band from mouth through eye to dorsal fin; large eye; 11 to 16 gill rakers on the lower limb of the first branchial arch

FISHING

Methods: trolling, drifting and casting

Bait: live and dead fish, squid and lures

Where: from deep water to the surface around wrecks and reefs

Tips: still-fish with live bait suspended above reefs; Pigfish work well as bait

GREATER AMBERJACK

Seriola dumerili

Other Names: jack, amberfish, horse-eyed bonito or jack

Habitat: offshore near bottom structure in 50 to 200 feet of water

Food: fish, crabs and squid

Reproduction: spawns in open water over reefs in late spring and early summer

Gulf Distribution: entire Gulf

Average Size: 10 to 20 pounds

World Record: 155 pounds, 12 ounces, Bermuda, 1992

Table Quality: good to excellent, but not often eaten in US; often has tapeworms encysted in the meat that are harmless to people

Notes: The Greater Amberjack is a premier sport fish throughout its range. This is a fast, hard-fighting fish that dives deep and tries to stay there. Amberjacks often travel in small schools, but are just as likely to be found as individuals. Greater Amberjacks concentrate around bottom structure but can be caught anywhere in the water column from the bottom to the surface. Amberjacks are fine table fare, but have been associated with ciguatera poisoning in the Caribbean and are not often eaten in the Gulf region.

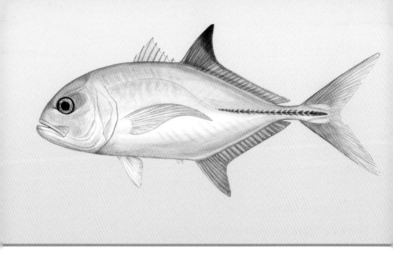

Description: body is evenly curved above and below; blue-gray back and silver sides; small black spot on edge of gill; lateral line arches in the front half of the fish; protruding sharp scales (scutes) along straight half of lateral line; yellow tail; other fins bluish black

FISHING

Methods: casting, trolling and drifting

Bait: small fish, live shrimp, lures and flies

Where: off beaches, reefs and channels offshore

Tips: once Horse-eye Jacks are spotted in a channel, silver spoons are very productive

HORSE-EYE JACK

Caranx latus

Other Names: big-eye jack, goggle-eye, horse-eye trevally

Habitat: offshore islands; reef and deep blue-water holes; beaches and channels inshore

Food: fish, squid and crabs

Reproduction: spawns in open water over reefs in early summer

Gulf Distribution: the entire Gulf

Average Size: 2 to 3 pounds

World Record: 29 pounds, 8 ounces, South Pacific, 1995

Table Quality: edible but seldom eaten

Notes: The Horse-eye Jack is a small jack that lives up to the jack family's hard-fighting reputation; it is fast and a good fighter, and it pulls hard to get to the bottom and tries to stay there. Horse-eye Jacks form small, tight schools that can provide some very fast action once located. Horse-eye Jacks are mostly an offshore species but on occasion they will enter the brackish water in rivers or large channels. Small schools of Horse-eye Jacks often frequent deep blue-water holes in sand flats. The Horse-eye Jack is not considered as tasty as other jack species and is seldom kept for the table.

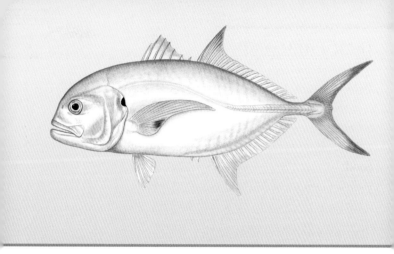

Description: deep body; greenish-gold back, silver sides and yellow belly; steep forehead; large mouth; dark oval spot on gill cover; dark spot on side extending to base of pectoral fin; crescent-shaped tail

FISHING

Methods: trolling, casting and drifting

Bait: live fish and shrimp, jigs and lures

Where: inshore waters near deeper jetties and reefs; channels and streams

Tips: use live fish or cast spinner baits along deep seawalls

82

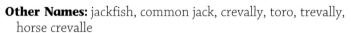

JACK CREVALLE
Caranx hippos

Other Names: jackfish, common jack, crevally, toro, trevally, horse crevalle

Habitat: brackish inshore bays and rivers; reefs and platforms just offshore

Food: fish, squid, crabs and shrimp

Reproduction: spawns over nearshore reefs throughout the summer

Gulf Distribution: entire Gulf

Average Size: 2 to 5 pounds

World Record: 58 pounds, 6 ounces, Angola, 2000

Table Quality: dark meat is strongly flavored; it is best prepared on the grill with lots of lime juice, smoked

Notes: The Jack Crevalle is one of the most abundant and widespread jack species found in the Gulf. Jack Crevalles can withstand a wide range of salinity levels and may show up in almost any coastal waters. As with other jacks, they are popular with fishermen for their hard, sustained fights but not for their food value. Smaller Jack Cravelles are often found in schools but larger fish usually travel alone. Crevalles prefer the liveliest baits and fast-moving lures. Fishing deep seawalls or harbor jetties can be very productive at times.

Description: very flat and deep, iridescent silver body; deep, narrow head with a very steep forehead (1½ times deep as long); long lobes on dorsal and anal fins, small pelvic fins

FISHING

> **Methods:** casting and still-fishing
>
> **Bait:** small live fish and shrimp, lures
>
> **Where:** docks, piers and jetties
>
> **Tips:** fish a small white or yellow jig tipped with a shrimp under bridge lights at night

LOOKDOWN

Selene vomer

Other Names: horsehead, silver flatfish

Habitat: shallow coastal waters (less than 40 ft) over a hard bottom

Food: shrimp, crabs and small fish

Reproduction: spawns on rocky shallows throughout the summer

Gulf Distribution: entire Gulf

Average Size: 6 to 10 inches, under a pound

World Record: 4 pounds, 10 ounces, Flamingo, Florida, 2004

Table Quality: excellent panfish; roll in corn muffin mix and fry

Notes: Lookdowns are funny-looking fish that are common in the shallow waters throughout the Gulf. They get their name from their tendency to swim on their sides as they look for food near the bottom. Lookdowns tend to congregate under the lights on docks and piers. They are very good fighters on light tackle, pulling hard while swimming in tight circles. Lookdowns prefer live bait or small, shiny lures and jigs fished near the bottom. The flesh has an excellent flavor and can't be beat when breaded and pan-fried.

Description: deep, flat body (narrower in larger fish); blue-gray back fading to silver sides and yellowish belly; blunt nose and small mouth; anal and dorsal fins are similar in size and appearance; pelvic and tail fins are yellowish

FISHING

Methods: still-fishing, casting and drifting

Bait: sand fleas, small crabs, jigs and shrimp

Where: surf, piers and jetties

Tips: use two hooks, one with shrimp, the other with a long piece of clam

FLORIDA POMPANO
Trachinotus carolinus

Jack Family

Carangidae

Other Names: common or Carolina pompano

Habitat: shallow inshore waters (often in the surf) with a sand or shell bottom

Food: mostly shellfish, clams (coquinas), mussels, crabs and shrimp

Reproduction: spawns just offshore in the open sea off and on throughout the summer

Gulf Distribution: the entire Gulf

Average Size: 1 to 2 pounds

World Record: 8 pounds, 4 ounces, Port St. Joe Bay, Florida, 1999

Table Quality: excellent; best baked or grilled whole with the skin on

Notes: This small jack species is best known for its fine-textured flesh with exceptional flavor. Commercially harvested and sold in restaurants, it is one of the most expensive fish on the market per pound. Florida Pompanos travel in small to very large schools, mostly inshore, but occasionally they are found just offshore at the mouth of channels. They are easy to catch with a small white, yellow or chartreuse jig and a piece of clam during their infrequent runs, but most of the time they are hard to locate. Pompanos feed on small mollusks and crustaceans, which they reportedly dig out of the sand. Pompanos have a very tough hide that makes them hard to clean, so they are best cooked whole and unskinned.

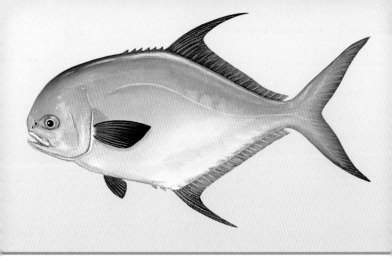

Description: round laterally compressed body with blunt
  snout; silver sides, often with a circular black area at the
  base of the pectoral fin; dark blue-green back; back dorsal
  fin has 1 spine and 17 to 19 soft rays (22 to 27 in Florida
  Pompano)

FISHING

Methods: casting, still-fishing

Bait: lures, flies, crab or clam meat, and shrimp

Where: flats with soft bottom

Tips: on the flats, stir up the bottom by working a small
  silver Johnson spoon tipped with a small crab

PERMIT

Trachinotus falcatus

Other Names: round, great or king pompano

Habitat: surf, channels, bays, grass and mud flats in warm water less than 100 feet deep

Food: crustaceans, mollusks and sea urchins

Reproduction: little is known of its life history

Gulf Distribution: present throughout the Gulf but much more common in southern warm waters

Average Size: 10 to 20 pounds

World Record: 60 pounds, Brazil

Table Quality: excellent when under 5 pounds

Notes: Permits are hard-fighting jacks that are an important sport fish in the warmer parts of the Gulf. They are often sought along with Bonefish by poling through the shallows in a flats boat; such anglers "hunt" for feeding fish and then cast toward them. They can also be caught if still-fished in channels near open flats and in the surf. Smaller Permits are frequently caught in the surf and are often confused with the Florida Pompano, which looks and taste similar.

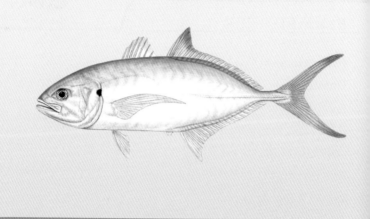

Description: body not as deep and more rounded than other
jacks; dark olive to bluish back (older fish are almost black);
sides silver to bronze; dark spot on edge of gill flap; arched
portion of lateral line short; black tips on tail and dorsal fins

FISHING

Methods: trolling, drifting, casting and still-fishing

Bait: live shrimp, small fish and cut bait

Where: just offshore

Tips: any shiny lure after a school is located

90

Carangidae

BLUE RUNNER
Caranx crysos

Other Names: hard-tailed or blue jack, hardtail

Habitat: open waters offshore

Food: fish, shrimp and squid

Reproduction: spawns offshore from January to midsummer

Gulf Distribution: entire Gulf

Average Size: 1 to 2 pounds

World Record: 11 pounds, 2 ounces, Dauphin Island, Alabama, 1997

Table Quality: very good; prized in some areas but disliked in others; it is best smoked or grilled with lots of lime juice

Notes: The Blue Runner is a small jack that gathers in large schools in open water just offshore. A few larger individuals are caught over reefs and small ones near floating vegetation. Along parts of the Atlantic Coast they are prized as a food fish and there is an active commercial market. Where there is a commercial market, Blue Runners are sold fresh and salted. They are not very popular as a food fish along the Gulf Coast, but throughout their range Blue Runners are a popular bait-fish for offshore big-game species.

Description: olive-gray body with tough, leathery skin; small terminal mouth with strong teeth; rear dorsal fin and anal fin similar in shape and marbled; soft dorsal fin has a long filament at its peak; lobes of anal fin extended in large fish

FISHING

Methods: still-fishing and drifting

Bait: shrimp, clams and cut bait

Where: docks and jetties inshore, reefs, wrecks and platforms offshore

Tips: use a very sharp long shank hook with a small piece of clam

GRAY TRIGGERFISH

Balistes capriscus

Balistidae

Other Names: common or dusky triggerfish

Habitat: near hard bottom structure in shallow coastal waters and offshore

Food: shellfish, sea urchins, barnacles and mussels

Reproduction: spawns offshore in spring through summer; eggs are deposited in a guarded nest

Gulf Distribution: entire Gulf

Average Size: 1 to 2 pounds

World Record: 13 pounds, 9 ounces, Murrells Inlet, South Carolina, 1989

Table Quality: very good to excellent, but hard to clean; bake or grill whole

Notes: The Gray Triggerfish is one of the most common and widespread triggerfish found in the Gulf. In the northern Gulf they are mostly caught offshore on reefs, over wrecks and under oil platforms; in the southern Gulf, they are frequently caught near jetties and docks. Triggerfish are named for their first dorsal spine, which locks in place and sticks straight up. The second dorsal spine must be pushed down or "triggered" to release the first spine. Triggerfish have a hard mouth full of sharp, stout teeth. They are hard to hook and good at nipping off fishing line and biting careless anglers.

Description: flattened body with eyes on top (left side);
olive-brown back with three "eye" spots; two of the eye
spots occur just above one another, the other is toward the
tail, just below lateral line in rear; white spots scattered
over body

FISHING

> **Methods:** still-fishing, casting, drifting and gigging
> (spearing)
>
> **Bait:** live shrimp and fish, cut bait and lures
>
> **Where:** docks, jetties, surf, channels and sand flats
>
> **Tips:** bump a yellow jig tipped with a live minnow on the
> bottom in sandy creeks and channels

GULF FLOUNDER
Paralichthys albigutta

Other Names: doormat, pile, sand flounder

Habitat: shallow inshore waters with a sandy, rocky or rubble bottom

Food: shrimp, crabs and fish

Reproduction: spawning takes place offshore in fall and winter

Gulf Distribution: entire Gulf

Average Size: 1 to 2 pounds

World Record: 6 pounds, 4 ounces, Dauphin Island, Alabama, 1996

Table Quality: excellent; dip in beer batter and deep fry

Notes: The Gulf Flounder is a small flounder that is common throughout the Gulf. Due to its small size, it is not as popular with sport or commercial fishermen as the Southern Flounder, but its flesh is firm, white and just as tasty. The Gulf Flounder prefers shallow water with a hard bottom, as opposed to the Southern Flounder, which prefers a muddy bottom in deep water. Gulf Flounders are often caught over sand and rubble near bridges and jetties. Both flounder species begin life by swimming upright with an eye on each side. As the fish matures, the right eye migrates to the left side and the fish rests on its right side.

Description: flattened body with eyes on top (left side); top is dark to light brown with dark spots and blotches that do not have black centers; fins are mottled

FISHING

Methods: still-fishing, drifting, casting and gigging (spearing)

Bait: live shrimp and fish, cut bait and lures

Where: bays, estuaries, channels and streams

Tips: use a fiddler crab with a small float a few inches from the hook, so the crab floats just off the bottom

SOUTHERN FLOUNDER

Paralichthys lethostigma

Other Names: mud flounder, pile, brown flatfish, southern fluke, halibut

Habitat: soft bottomed shallows during warm weather; just offshore in winter, streams and channels

Food: fish, crabs and shrimp

Reproduction: spawning takes place offshore in fall and winter

Gulf Distribution: entire Gulf

Average Size: 12 to 24 inches, 2 to 6 pounds

World Record: 20 pounds, 9 ounces, Nassau, Florida, 1982

Table Quality: excellent; stuff with shrimp or crab and bake

Notes: The Southern Flounder is a popular sport fish throughout its range. There are also large commercial fisheries for flounders in many Gulf states. Southern Flounders can withstand a wide range of salinity levels and are often caught many miles up freshwater streams during the summer. The Southern Flounder's preference for soft bottoms has earned it the name of "mud flounder" in many regions. Like other members of the Left-eyed Flatfish family, young Southern Flounders have an eye on each side of their head, and as the fish matures the right eye migrates to the left side and the fish lays on its right side. In a separate family of flounders, the eye migrates to the right-hand side.

Description: long, narrow body; brownish sides with a blue-green back; 8 diamond-shaped orange blotches on sides; very pointed snout; large mouth with many small teeth; one soft dorsal fin and one adipose fin

FISHING

Methods: still-fishing and drifting

Bait: live or cut bait

Where: shallow coastal water over a soft bottom

Tips: use a large white jig with a small strip of cut fish

INSHORE LIZARDFISH
Synodus foetens

Other Names: snakefish, sand or lizard pike

Habitat: salty and brackish bays and estuaries with a mud bottom

Food: fish, shrimp

Reproduction: little is known of their natural history

Gulf Distribution: entire Gulf

Average Size: 12 to 15 inches

World Record: none

Table Quality: not often eaten, but reportedly has a good flavor

Notes: The Inshore Lizardfish is common to all the shallow waters of the Gulf and is considered a real nuisance by most anglers. They are a bottom-dwelling fish that prefer a mud or soft sand bottom with little structure. Lizardfish lie on the bottom, then dart up to strike with greater force then their size would indicate. They will attack almost any bait and keep at it until they are hooked. The Lizardfish's small, sharp teeth may inflict a painful bite, but the fish is not venomous as has been reported. All fish smell bad when left in the sun but lizardfish can be particularly unpleasant.

Description: long, torpedo-shaped body; blue-gray back; silver sides with no spots, occasionally light or no stripes; front dorsal fin is blue (never black); lateral line drops steeply between the first and second dorsal fin; scaled pectoral fin

FISHING

Methods: trolling, drifting and still-fishing

Bait: live and rigged fish

Where: nearshore open Gulf, deepwater bridges and jetties

Tips: drift a rigged fish held up with a balloon off the stern of a party boat

Scombridae

KING MACKEREL
Scomberomorus cavalla

Other Names: kingfish, giant mackerel

Habitat: open Gulf often near wrecks or reefs, occasionally deeper inshore water of channels and rivers

Food: mostly fish, but they also eat small quantities of shrimp and squid

Reproduction: spawns far offshore in midsummer

Gulf Distribution: the southern Gulf in winter; the entire Gulf during the summer

Average Size: 15 to 20 pounds

World Record: 93 pounds, Puerto Rico, 1999

Table Quality: oily, but very good; best grilled or smoked

Notes: The King Mackerel is the largest mackerel species found in the Gulf and the most important as a sport and commercial fish. During the summer, King Mackerels are the most popular fish for charter boat fishing in the open Gulf. King Mackerels form large schools that are always moving, as the fish seek schools of prey. A species of the open Gulf for the most part, they do come close to shore on occasion, but never into turbid water. Like other mackerels, King Mackerels have dark, oily flesh revered by some and hated by others.

Description: streamlined torpedo-shaped body; bluish green back and silver sides; sides have bronze to yellow-brown spots without stripes; starting between the dorsal fins the lateral line curves evenly to tail; the first dorsal fin is black; no scales on pectoral fin

FISHING

Methods: trolling, drifting and still-fishing

Bait: lures and flies, live and cut fish, shrimp

Where: bays, estuaries to near offshore

Tips: a spinner on one of the new soft-bodied squid lures works very well

SPANISH MACKEREL

Scomberomorus maculatus

Other Names: breakfast mackerel

Habitat: open water of bays, estuaries and occasionally grassy flats; near offshore over reefs; smaller fish just outside surf line

Food: small fish, squid and shrimp

Reproduction: spawns in open sea from late spring throughout the summer

Gulf Distribution: the entire Gulf during warm months; the southern Gulf in winter

Average Size: 2 to 4 pounds

World Record: 13 pounds, Ocracoke Inlet, North Carolina, 1987

Table Quality: excellent; very good when smoked or grilled with lemon and garlic butter

Notes: This is one of the common mackerels of the Gulf Coast and it is considered a prime sport fish when fished with light spinning tackle or a fly rod. Spanish Mackerels travel in fast-moving schools that frequent the nearshore waters much more frequently than King Mackerels. They are occasionally caught from docks and jetties but much better luck is had in open water $\frac{1}{4}$ to 1 mile from these structures. There is a large commercial fishery for Spanish Mackerel on the East Coast and a small one in the Gulf.

Description: deep, torpedo-shaped body; bluish black back; silver-gray sides with a brownish yellow stripe on upper part; all finlets are dusky gray to black with white tips, never yellow; pectoral fin reaches back to the center of rear dorsal fin

FISHING

Methods: trolling, drifting and casting

Bait: lures, rigged and live fish, strip baits

Where: the open Gulf

Tips: high speed trolling is the key to Blackfin Tuna fishing

BLACKFIN TUNA

Thunnus atlanticus

Other Names: Bermuda tuna, blackfinned albacore, deep tunny

Habitat: open offshore Gulf waters

Food: fish, but also many small crustaceans like crabs, stomatopods and squid

Reproduction: spawns in open, clear water from spring through summer

Gulf Distribution: entire Gulf

Average Size: 5 to 15 pounds

World Record: 46 pounds, 6 ounces, Marathon, Florida, 2006

Table Quality: excellent; eaten raw or cooked; best broiled or grilled

Notes: The Blackfin Tuna is the most common true tuna in the Gulf and is very plentiful in the western Gulf during the summer. It is the most popular tuna with coastal fishermen, as it is plentiful, a hard fighter and great table fare. Blackfin Tuna are thought to eat more squid and crustaceans than other tuna, but they are still primarily fish eaters as adults. Like others species in the tuna family, Blackfins are an open-water species and are rarely seen near shore. Blackfin Tuna are frequently preyed upon by Blue Marlin and are popular marlin baitfish in some areas.

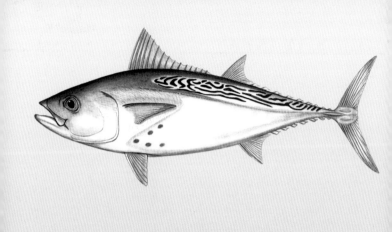

Description: shallow, torpedo-shaped body; steely blue back and silver sides with a metallic sheen; 4 or 5 dark spots below pectoral fin; dark, wavy bars on back above the lateral line from about the middle of the dorsal fin to tail

FISHING

Methods: trolling, drifting and casting

Bait: lures, rigged fish and small, live fish

Where: open water inshore and offshore; occasionally near bridges

Tips: nearshore flocks of diving birds can help anglers locate schools of feeding Little Tunny

Scombridae

LITTLE TUNNY
Euthynnus alletteratus

Other Names: false albacore, bonito

Habitat: open water from very close to shore to well offshore

Food: small crustaceans, squid and fish

Reproduction: spawns offshore in open seas throughout most of the year

Gulf Distribution: entire Gulf

Average Size: 8 to 10 pounds

World Record: 36 pounds, Washington Canyon, New Jersey, 2006

Table Quality: light meat is excellent; dark meat has a strong flavor and should be removed; more popular in the Caribbean and South America than in the US

Notes: The Little Tunny is often confused with the Bonito, but the bars on the Tunny's back and the spots under its pectoral fins make it easy to differentiate between the two. Little Tunnys are a schooling fish that travel and feed near the surface. Fishermen can often spot tunny by watching for flocks of birds, which congregate over feeding schools. Little Tunnys are great fighters, but not popular as food. Their flavor can be improved if they are bled and iced soon after landing and if any dark meat is removed before cooking.

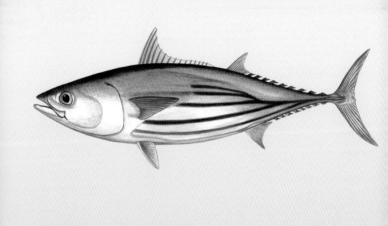

Description: torpedo-shaped body; back is dark bluish purple; lower sides silver with 3 to 5 bluish black horizontal stripes; dorsal fins connected at base; many small conical teeth

FISHING

Methods: trolling, drifting and casting

Bait: rigged and live fish, and lures

Where: offshore waters

Tips: troll at 8 to 10 knots near floating vegetation

SKIPJACK TUNA

Katsuwonus pelamis

Scombridae

Other Names: ocean or arctic bonito, striped or watermelon tuna

Habitat: deep open ocean

Food: fish, squid and crab larvae

Reproduction: spawns in open seas in early summer

Gulf Distribution: the entire Gulf in warm weather

Average Size: 3 to 10 pounds

World Record: 45 pounds, 4 ounces, Baja California, Mexico, 1996

Table Quality: good to excellent; dark meat with a strong flavor that is best grilled; commercially canned

Notes: The Skipjack Tuna and the Little Tunny are both small tuna species that are often mistakenly referred to as bonito. The true Bonito, *Sarda sarda*, is not very common in the Gulf and can be identified by the oblique stripes on its sides above the lateral line. Skipjack Tuna travel near the surface of the open Gulf in large schools of 50,000 or more fish. Tuna are voracious eaters and may consume a third of their weight in a day. When Skipjacks are located, anglers often circle the school casting spoons and jigs into the school for some fast, furious action.

Description: long, narrow body with a long pointed snout; steel blue back and silver-blue sides; 25 to 30 blue-black vertical bars on sides; large mouth with movable upper jaw and many sharp laterally flattened teeth; long, low front dorsal fin

FISHING

Methods: deep trolling

Bait: rigged fish, lures

Where: offshore in open Gulf

Tips: baits should always be shiny and moving in a straight line so this fast fish doesn't miss the strike

WAHOO

Acanthocybium solandri

Other Names: ocean barracuda, Pacific kingfish, pride of Bermuda, queenfish, tigerfish, oahu fish

Habitat: open ocean, often around reefs, wrecks and bottom breaks, bouys

Food: fish

Reproduction: spawns in open seas during early summer

Gulf Distribution: the entire Gulf, but more common in the southern Gulf

Average Size: 15 to 50 pounds

World Record: 184 pounds, Cabo San Lucas, Mexico, 2005

Table Quality: very good to excellent; best broiled or grilled

Notes: The Wahoo is one of the fastest fish in the ocean, reportedly swimming 50 miles per hour or more. This speed makes it a very exciting game fish, as it can remove hundreds of yards of line in a few seconds. Wahoo are also a great food fish and are particularly prized for some specialty dishes in Bermuda. Unlike the other mackerel species that often school, Wahoo are usually solitary or occur in small groups of only a few fish. The Wahoo also differs from other mackerels as it routinely feeds well below the surface.

Scombridae

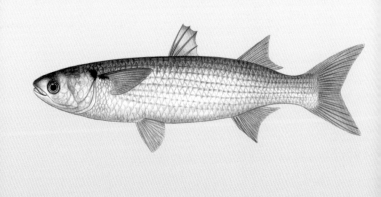

Description: long, narrow body with a blunt snout and a small mouth; blue-green or brown back; silver sides with scales that have a dark spot at the base forming conspicuous stripes; dorsal and anal fins unscaled; dark mark at base of pectoral fin

FISHING

Methods: cast netting and still-fishing

Bait: small bits of almost anything

Where: coastal shallows to freshwater streams

Tips: chumming with cornmeal can concentrate mullets

STRIPED MULLET

Mugil cephalus

Other Names: black or jumping mullet

Habitat: ubiquitous in shallow coastal waters; present in everything from waters with high salinity to well up freshwater streams

Food: mostly herbivorous, feeding on algae and detritus

Reproduction: spawns in open seas near inlets from fall through early winter

Gulf Distribution: entire Gulf

Average Size: 1 to 2 pounds

World Record: 7 pounds, 10 ounces, Buena Vista Lagoon, California, 2004

Table Quality: bony, but when caught in clear water, the flesh is excellent smoked or fried; the roe is also very good

Notes: The Striped Mullet is the most common large mullet species found throughout the Gulf. The White Mullet is smaller (under a pound) and lacks stripes on the sides and has scales on the dorsal and anal fins. Striped Mullets are commonly netted for both food and bait, but they are not often sought after by anglers. Fishing for mullet is usually done through cracks in docks and well up freshwater streams. They are tricky to catch, as mullet do not often eat the bait, they just mouth it, and anglers have to be quick to set the hook. In some parts of the Gulf, mullets are prized as food; in others, they taste muddy and are disdained.

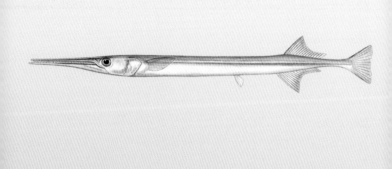

Description: long, narrow body; blue or blue-green back; large mouth with snout elongated into thin "needle"; lower jaw longer than upper jaw; side of head pale below eye; bluish tail

FISHING

Methods: casting, still-fishing and netting

Bait: small live shrimp and fish, cut baits, lures and flies

Where: docks and jetties in protected bays; freshwater streams

Tips: try a small shrimp with a spinner

ATLANTIC NEEDLEFISH

Belonidae

Strongylura marina

Other Names: needlegar, saltwater gar

Habitat: shallow, protected bays and estuaries to well up freshwater streams

Food: small fish

Reproduction: little is known of their natural history

Gulf Distribution: entire Gulf

Average Size: 18 to 24 inches; $\frac{1}{2}$ to 1 pound

World Record: 4 pounds, 1 ounce, Cape May Reel, New Jersey, 2004

Table Quality: edible, but bony and not often eaten in this country

Notes: Needlefish are voracious predators of small fish. The Atlantic Needlefish is the most common needlefish variety in the Gulf and can be found almost anywhere, from protected bays and estuaries to open water and even far up freshwater streams. Needlefish are a nuisance for inshore anglers, as they attack any bait fished near the surface, but they are popular as bait with offshore fishermen. Needlefish can be fun to catch with top-water lures and fly rods if the tackle is light enough. Once hooked, needlefish frequently dance across the water on their tails. In some parts of their range, they are fried crisp and eaten whole, but they are not often eaten in this country.

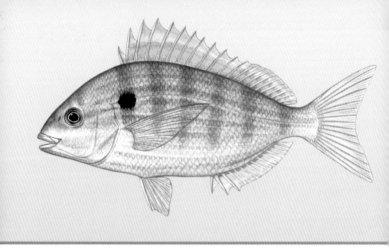

Description: deep body is flattened laterally; silver body with yellow and blue stripes and faint dark bars; dark round spot on lateral line just above the pectoral fin; small mouth; sharp spines on dorsal and anal fin

FISHING

Methods: still-fishing and drifting

Bait: small pieces of shrimp, squid, fish, clams and bloodworms.

Where: docks, piers and jetties; over reefs and sand flats

Tips: very small white jig ($1/_{64}$ ounce or less) tipped with squid tentacle

PINFISH

Sparidae

Lagodon rhomboides

Other Names: pin perch, bream, saltwater or sea bream, sailor's choice, Spanish porgy

Habitat: from inshore shallows with a hard bottom to wrecks and reefs just offshore

Food: worms, crustaceans and mollusks

Reproduction: spawns just offshore in late fall through early winter

Gulf Distribution: entire Gulf

Average Size: 6 to 10 inches

World Record: 3 pounds, 5 ounces, Horn Island, Mississippi, 1992

Table Quality: a respectable panfish if large enough

Notes: The Pinfish is a common and well-known fish of the Gulf that may show up in almost any body of water, no matter whether it is salty or brackish. They are a frequent bait robber that often trouble dock and jetty fishermen. They are often not large enough to take home, but when they are, they are excellent breaded and fried whole like other panfish. A small jig tipped with a piece of clam fished in deep holes along jetties is an effective method for catching larger Pinfish. Pinfish are a popular baitfish (whether dead or alive) and are often used over reefs and wrecks when fishing for larger predators like groupers or snappers.

Description: deep body with a steep-sloping forehead; iridescent bluish silver body; deeply forked tail; knobbed tubercle above nostril

FISHING

Methods: still-fishing and drifting

Bait: small crabs, sand fleas and cut bait

Where: reefs and wrecks

Tips: use a strong leader or a long, shanked hook or it will get nipped off; sea urchin meat is a great bait

KNOBBED PORGY
Calamus nodosus

Other Names: Key West or clown porgy

Habitat: near the bottom in 20 to 300 feet of water near hard structure

Food: crabs, clams, starfish and sea urchins

Reproduction: matures at 4 or 5 years then spawns in the open sea from May through June

Gulf Distribution: primarily the eastern Gulf from western Louisiana; occasionally caught in southern Texas Gulf

Average Size: 1 to 2 pounds

World Record: 5 pounds, 2 ounces, Texas, 2000

Table Quality: excellent flavor; stuff with shrimp and bake for a real treat

Notes: The Knobbed Porgy is one the largest porgy species and certainly the most colorful. They are marketed commercially in small numbers, but most are caught by sport fishermen. Knobbed Porgies are most frequently caught when fishing in deep water for snappers or groupers. In the Keys, they are occasionally caught from bridges that cross deep water and have rocky structure on the bottom. Knobbed Porgies are a bottom-dwelling species with strong incisors and molars for crushing shellfish and are good at clipping off hooks that are not attached to a strong leader.

Description: deep bluish silver body; dark irregular blotches on sides; steep, sloping forehead and somewhat pointed purplish gray snout; large mouth; blue lines above and below eye

FISHING

Methods: still-fishing and drifting

Bait: cut bait, crabs and shrimp

Where: reefs and wrecks

Tips: bait with small crabs on a strong hook

WHITEBONE PORGY

Calamus leucosteus

Other Names: white or silver porgy, silver or slip snapper

Habitat: deep water with significant structure, like rocks, reef or wrecks

Food: crabs, shrimp, snails and sea urchins

Reproduction: matures at 1 to 2 years; spawns on deep reefs in late spring to early summer

Gulf Distribution: entire Gulf

Average Size: 1 to 2 pounds

World Record: 3 pounds, 5 ounces, Orange Beach, Alabama, 2003

Table Quality: bony, but flesh has a good texture, meat can be dry, so it is best prepared fried or poached

Notes: The Whitebone Porgy is a fish species that is commonly caught by party boat anglers anchored over reefs that have a lot of structure or wrecks. Porgies seem to be easier to catch than snappers and put up somewhat less of a fight when they are hooked. The flesh is a little dry, but it has a good flavor and is sometimes marketed as silver snapper. The Whitebone Porgy is one of those curious fish that is a protogynous hermaphrodite (many of the females change sex as they mature), so all larger fish are males.

Description: deep, laterally compressed body; silver to dusky yellow body with black vertical bands; 6 or 7 bands are present in fish from the eastern Gulf; 5 bands are present in fish from the western Gulf; fins black; flat teeth protruding from mouth

FISHING

Methods: still-fishing

Bait: fiddler crabs, barnacles and sand fleas

Where: docks, piers and bridges

Tips: chumming with crushed oysters or crabs will attract Sheepsheads

SHEEPSHEAD

Archosargus probatocephalus

Other Names: convict fish, crabeater, sheepshead seabream

Habitat: shallow bays, estuaries and brackish streams near barnacle-covered structures

Food: shellfish, sea urchins and barnacles

Reproduction: spawns in late spring and summer along sandy shores and beaches

Gulf Distribution: entire Gulf

Average Size: 2 to 4 pounds

World Record: 21 pounds, 4 ounces, New Orleans, Louisiana, 1982

Table Quality: excellent baked, broiled or grilled

Notes: The Sheepshead is a popular sport fish throughout its range and is commercially harvested in many areas. It gets its name from the flat teeth that protrude from its mouth and look somewhat like a sheep's teeth. They use their teeth very effectively, biting barnacles off of rocks and nipping the hooks from anglers' lines. Sheepsheads are plentiful around docks and jetties and can be caught with crabs or sand fleas fished on the bottom or dangled from piers or bridge abutments. They are good fighters when hooked, making several strong, short runs.

Description: elongated, diamond-shaped body; gray-green above; pale yellow below; yellowish tan round and crescent-shaped spots on sides; snout long; eyes set high on sloping forehead; squared tail

FISHING

Methods: still-fishing and drifting

Bait: shrimp, squid and cut baits

Where: docks, jetties and grass flats with rocks

Tips: the best puffer fishing is on the rocky edges of grass flats

SOUTHERN PUFFER

Sphoeroides nephelus

Other Names: blowfish, toadfish

Habitat: widespread around rocks and reefs in shallow, protected bays and estuaries; less common on mud or grassy flats; will enter brackish water and freshwater streams

Food: crabs, clams, mussels and sea urchins

Reproduction: matures in 1 year; in spring through early summer, females lay clumps of gelatinous eggs that attach to the bottom

Gulf Distribution: entire Gulf

Average Size: 6 to 10 inches

World Record: none

Table Quality: the flesh is reported to be good, but the skin and entrails are poisonous; in many areas they were overharvested during food rationing in WWII

Notes: The Southern Puffer is probably the most common puffer species in the Gulf. They tolerate a wide range of habitats and may be caught anywhere in shallow coastal waters, even in freshwater streams. Like other puffer species, they can inflate with water to become much larger and rounder, making it harder for larger predators to swallow them. Southern Puffers are persistent bait robbers, picking at even large baits until hooked. The Southern Puffer's skin and entrails are poisonous, so this small fish is probably not worth trying to eat. Small Puffers can be kept in an aquarium by adding a little table salt to the water.

Description: long, flattened body; back dusky gray or brown; snout long and saw-like (¹/₄ body length) with 24 or more teeth on each side; first dorsal fin entirely above pelvic fin

FISHING

This rare species is occasionally caught when fishing the bottom with cut baits or live fish, but should not be targeted. When sawfish are caught, they should not be removed from the water and the line should be cut a few inches from the mouth.

SMALLTOOTH SAWFISH
Pristis pectinata

Other Names: none

Habitat: shallow bays and estuaries with a muddy or soft sand bottom; freshwater streams

Food: small fish and crabs

Reproduction: gives birth to live young

Gulf Distribution: primarily the northern Gulf

Average Size: 3 to 4 feet

World Record: none

Table Quality: reportedly good

Notes: The Smalltooth Sawfish is the sawfish most commonly found in the northern Gulf. The Largetooth Sawfish is a tropical species and only ventures north in warm weather. Both are now very rare in most of the gulf and protected, but there is still a good population of Smalltooth Sawfish in southern Florida. Sawfish are closely related to stingrays; in fact, they are elongated rays. Sawfish give birth to live young that are about 2 feet long; the young sawfish are born with their saws in a sheath to protect the mother. Both fish readily enter fresh water and may travel many miles upstream. They use their saws to extract small fish from the mud or use them to slash through schooled fish. They are not aggressive and are not dangerous to people unless handled.

Description: stout brownish green body; body and fins covered with reddish brown spots that get larger toward the belly; three dark shadows under dorsal fin; whitish margin on tail and anal fin; mouth large

FISHING

Methods: still-fishing and drifting

Bait: cut baits, crabs and squid

Where: jetties and shallow rock structure out to the shelf break

Tips: squid or crabs seem to outperform cut fish

ROCK HIND
Epinephelus adscensionis

Other Names: grouper, jack, rock cod

Habitat: shallow rocky structure out to deeper reefs

Food: fish, crabs, shrimp and squid

Reproduction: female Rock Hinds turn into males as they grow larger (such species are called protogynous hermaphrodites); spawning occurs at 3 years of age in the open sea near reefs

Gulf Distribution: the entire Gulf; more plentiful in the southern Gulf

Average Size: 1 to 2 pounds

World Record: 9 pounds, South Pacific, 1994

Table Quality: white, flaky meat with good flavor; good baked or fried

Notes: Like other species in its family, this brightly colored fish can change colors from dark to light to match its surroundings. As its name suggests, Rock Hinds prefer a rock substrate and can be found around jetties, breakwaters and reefs. Rock Hinds inhabit a variety of depths, from inshore shallows out to the reefs on the snapper grounds. Though the Rock Hind is a solitary fish, when a good spot is found, many of them can be caught. Rock Hinds have a large mouth and often engulf very large chunks of cut bait with a voracious strike and then put up little fight while being landed.

Description: long body for a grouper; pale to dark gray or gray-brown body; many dark wormlike markings on entire body; pelvic, anal and tail fins blackish with blue or white edges; often with a black mustache over mouth

FISHING

Methods: still-fishing and drifting

Bait: live and cut fish, crabs and lures

Where: deep inshore holes and grass flats; offshore reefs and wrecks

Tips: look for an 8-to-12-foot bottom ridge in 80 to 180 feet of water

GAG

Mycteroperca microlepis

Other Names: gray, black, gag or grass grouper, charcoal belly

Habitat: deep holes, ledges and grass flats near shore; older fish frequent reefs and wrecks offshore

Food: fish, crabs and squid

Reproduction: matures between 5 and 7 years of age, spawns from January through spring in open seas near offshore reefs

Gulf Distribution: entire Gulf

Average Size: 1 to 3 pounds

World Record: 80 pounds, 8 ounces, Destin, Florida, 1993

Table Quality: excellent, with white, flaky flesh; best when stuffed and baked

Notes: The Gag is a common grouper and is closely related to the Black Grouper, with which it is often confused. Young Gags are often found inshore in deep holes with ledges and along deep grass flats, particularly if there is some rock cover nearby. Older, larger fish move to reefs and rocks off-shore. Twenty pound Gags were once fairly common but are now rare, due to overharvesting. Like some other groupers, Gags have deeply embedded scales that make them hard to clean. The meat is very good and is well worth the effort.

Description: dark brown to lighter brownish green body; 4 or 5 irregular pale brown bands across body; many blackish brown spots on head and fins; large mouth extends past eye; the 3rd through the 11th dorsal spines are about the same length

FISHING

Methods: still-fishing and drifting

Bait: large live or dead fish

Where: near shore channels and river mouths with rocky hiding places, offshore gaps and breaks in deep water

Tips: in the southern Gulf, deep channels under bridges still produce a few Goliath Groupers

GOLIATH GROUPER

Epinephelus itajara

Other Names: giant grouper, Jewfish, Florida, spotted, great or southern Jewfish

Habitat: jetties, rock ledges, wrecks and reefs 100 to 150 feet deep

Food: crabs, fish and squid, all of which are eaten whole

Reproduction: little is known of their natural history

Gulf Distribution: the entire Gulf; more common in the southern Gulf

Average Size: 40 to 140 pounds

World Record: 680 pounds, Fernandina Beach, Florida, 1961

Table Quality: excellent at all sizes

Notes: The Goliath Grouper is the largest member of the family with 200- and 300-pound fish being fairly common. Unlike many of the larger groupers, Goliaths are a near-shore species and are often found in less than 100 feet of water. Forty years ago in the Florida Keys it was not uncommon for a bridge fisherman to catch a 400 pound monster, they are now quite rare, as their easy accessibility and great food value made them prime targets for many fishermen. They are now highly regulated in many areas.

Description: stout, reddish brown body; scattered white spots over pale blotches; small black spots around mouth; inside of mouth red or orange; hard dorsal fin high with a straight edge; pectoral fins longer than pelvic fins; dorsal, anal and tail fins blackish with white margins

FISHING

Methods: still-fishing and drifting

Bait: live fish, crabs, squid and cut baits

Where: rock ledges and wrecks

Tips: fish a small squid by bringing it up several feet then dropping it back to the bottom

RED GROUPER

Epinephelus morio

Serranidae

Other Names: mero americano

Habitat: rock walls, ledges and wrecks from 20 to 300 feet deep

Food: crabs, shrimp, lobsters, octopus and fish

Reproduction: matures in 4 to 7 years, then spawns in the open sea

Gulf Distribution: the entire Gulf

Average Size: 5 to 10 pounds

World Record: 42 pounds, 2 ounces, St. Augustine, Florida, 1997

Table Quality: good to excellent when baked or grilled with lime juice and butter

Notes: The Red Grouper is a large, stout fish closely related to the Nassau Grouper. They are solitary fish that can be found in any water from 10 to 300 feet deep, but they need holes and crevices to hide in. Rock walls, ledges and wrecks are good Red Grouper habitat. Red groupers are a favorite target of spearfishermen in many clear water areas and have been severely overharvested. They are strong fighters when hooked and quick action is needed to keep them from returning to their holes and cutting the line.

Description: large, heavy body; body uniformly grayish
  brown; dark stripe from snout through eye to back; 4 to 5
  blotchy bars on sides; 10 dorsal spines; the second spine is
  very long; black spots around eye; square tail

FISHING

Methods: still-fishing and drifting

Bait: large whole and cut fish

Where: seabed valleys and steep drop-offs well offshore

Tips: live porgies and snappers are the best baits for big
  Warsaw Groupers

WARSAW GROUPER

Hyporthodus

Other Names: black grouper or Jewfish, giant or great grouper

Habitat: steep drop-offs and cuts in greater than 100 feet of water for large fish; small fish prefer jetties and channels in inland bays

Food: crabs, lobsters and fish

Reproduction: little is known of reproduction

Gulf Distribution: the entire Gulf; more common in the northern Gulf

Average Size: 20 to 30 pounds

World Record: 436 pounds, 12 ounces, Gulf of Mexico, Florida, 1985

Table Quality: excellent when small; larger fish make great chowders and stews

Notes: The Warsaw Grouper is the second largest grouper found in the Gulf, the Goliath Grouper being the largest. Warsaw Groupers prefer cooler water than Goliath Groupers and are more common in the northern Gulf and they may move to slightly shallower water during the winter. They are an open Gulf fish that inhabits deep water from 100 to over 1,000 feet. Warsaw Groupers are bottom-dwellers that hang along steep ledges and in cuts in the sea floor.

Description: elongated grouper body; tan body with dark spots grouped in oval clusters; broom-like tail with long outer lobes and a rough edge

FISHING

Methods: still-fishing and drifting

Bait: live or cut fish, squid

Where: snapper banks

Tips: evening and night are the best times to fish for scamps

SCAMP
Mycteroperca phenax

Other Names: brown, scamp or broomtail grouper

Habitat: prefers a live coral bottom 40 to 250 feet deep; occasionally congregates over wrecks or reefs

Food: crabs, shrimp and fish

Reproduction: at about 3 years old, scamps spawn in open seas; like other groupers, the young float at the surface for several days before settling to the bottom

Gulf Distribution: the entire Gulf; more common in the north

Average Size: 4 to 6 pounds

World Record: 29 pounds, 10 ounces, Dauphin Island, Alabama, 2000

Table Quality: excellent with a fine flavor when fried or grilled

Notes: The Scamp is a very popular grouper that is found in shallow to moderately deep water. Scamps generally avoid the steep structure and hideaways that other grouper species favor; instead, Scamps prefer to swim over live coral or a shell bottom. If Scamps are found around wrecks or rock ledges they a likely to be in small schools just above the structure. Scamps are prized by sport fishermen for their hard strikes and hard, pulling fight. As one of the best-tasting grouper species, Scamps are highly sought after by both sport and commercial fishermen.

Description: stout body with a high back and a flattened head; bluish black to brown body; pale centers of scales form faint stripes on sides; elongated top ray on tail; sharp spine on gill cover

FISHING

Methods: still-fishing and drifting

Bait: shrimp, cut bait

Where: piers, jetties, wrecks and reefs

Tips: fish white jigs tipped with cut bait 2 feet above the bottom

GULF BLACK SEA BASS

Centropristis striata

Other Names: humpback, pin sea bass, rock bass, black fish, black will

Habitat: smaller fish found in shallow inshore waters with hard structure; larger fish are found offshore around reefs and wrecks down to about 200 feet

Food: clams, shrimp, crabs and small fish

Reproduction: long spawning season from June to October; females lay 30,000 to 50,000 eggs in open water over a hard bottom

Gulf Distribution: the northeastern Gulf

Average Size: 1 to 2 pounds

World Record: 10 pounds, 4 ounces; Virginia Beach, Virginia, 2000

Table Quality: excellent; some think Sea Bass has the finest flavor of all marine fish

Notes: The Gulf Black Sea Bass is a small member of the Sea Bass family that is mainly caught from the Florida Panhandle to the Mississippi River. Their reputation as fine table fare makes them very popular on the East Coast with sport and commercial fishermen alike. They are not as popular in the Gulf. Small Black Sea Bass are a common catch around rocky structures in protected bays and estuaries. The larger fish move out to deeper wrecks and reefs. Black Sea Bass are protogynous hermaphrodites (fish that change sexes as they age) and all large fish are males.

141

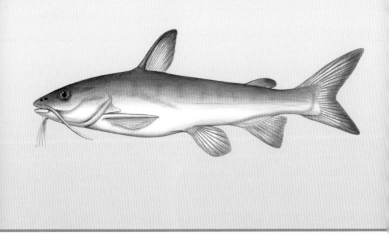

Description: elongated body tapering to a forked tail; blue-gray head and back fading to silver sides; 6 barbels around mouth; barbels at corner of mouth reach pectoral fins; sharp, locking spines in dorsal and pectoral fins

FISHING

   Methods: still-fishing

   Bait: shrimp, cut baits

   Where: jetties, bridges and piers

   Tips: small wire hooks can be made to remove hardheads without touching them; ask locals for instructions

HARDHEAD CATFISH
Ariopsis felis

Other Names: sea or marine catfish, seacat, tourist trout

Habitat: any shallow nearshore waters with a soft bottom, can withstand high turbidity and low salinity

Food: small crustaceans, worms and plant matter

Reproduction: spawns in bays and inlets during summer; male broods eggs in mouth

Gulf Distribution: entire Gulf

Average Size: 6 to 8 inches, under a pound

World Record: 3 pounds, 5 ounces, Sebastian, Florida, 1993

Table Quality: edible, but not often eaten

Notes: The Hardhead Catfish is one of the real pests plaguing inshore fishing in the entire Gulf. This persistent bait robber is so plentiful in some areas that there is little time for other more desirable fish to take the bait. To add insult to injury, the dorsal and pectoral spines are venomous and being poked by one can bring tears to the eyes of the toughest angler. Luckily, uttering a few strong words, washing in seawater, and then applying antiseptic will bring relief.

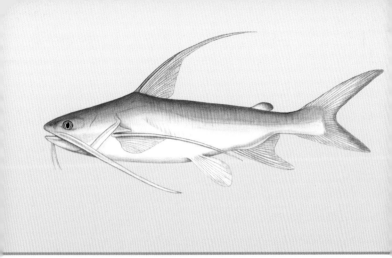

Description: stout body with a large head tapering to tail; steel gray back and silver sides and belly; locking spines in pectoral and dorsal fins that end in long filaments; 4 barbels near mouth; the lower barbel is flattened and extends to the anal fin

FISHING

> **Methods:** still-fishing and drifting
>
> **Bait:** live and cut fish
>
> **Where:** docks, jetties and bridges
>
> **Tips:** will readily strike a white jig tipped with cut fish that is bumped along the bottom

GAFFTOPSAIL CATFISH

Bagre marinus

Other Names: bandera, sailboat, sail and gaftop catfish

Habitat: shallow bays and estuaries in warm weather; deeper holes or near offshore waters in winter

Food: shrimp, squid and fish

Reproduction: little is known about reproduction but is thought to be a mouth breeder

Gulf Distribution: the entire Gulf

Average Size: 2 to 3 pounds

World Record: 10 pounds, Boca Raton, Florida, 2007

Table Quality: very good when breaded and fried

Notes: The Gafftopsail Catfish is a very common inhabitant of protected waters throughout the Gulf States. They are often found around docks in marinas, particularly near fish cleaning stations. Gafftops have a mixed reputation depending on where they are caught. In the southeastern Gulf they are not popular and rarely eaten. In parts of Texas they are prized as table fare. They are easy to catch when fished on the bottom with cut and live bait. The large spines in the dorsal and pectoral fins are venomous and can give a nasty sting.

Description: elongated body; greenish to brownish gray back; wide, expanded head swept back with a notched front margin; high dorsal fin sometimes with a black tip; top lobe of tail is extended

FISHING

Methods: still-fishing and drifting

Bait: live and cut fish, squid

Where: bridges, surf and just offshore

Tips: deep water at the edge of grass flats is a good area for sharks

SCALLOPED HAMMERHEAD SHARK
Sphyrna lewini

Other Names: notched hammerhead

Habitat: seabed; from inshore shallows to offshore reefs

Food: squid, octopus, lobsters, bottom fish and stingrays

Reproduction: matures at 5 to 7 feet; in spring gives birth to 15 to 30 pups after a 10-month gestation period

Gulf Distribution: the entire Gulf; more common in the southern Gulf

Average Size: 6 to 10 feet

World Record: 353 pounds; Key West, Florida, 2004

Table Quality: good as far as shark meat goes; sharks are marketed commercially in the Caribbean and South America; best when grilled with lime juice

Notes: The curious flattened head of the hammerhead family of sharks makes them easy to identify. The purpose for the wide head is unclear, but it could be an adaptation for better maneuverability while swimming near the bottom or a mechanism that helps them locate prey more effectively. Both theories may be true. Scalloped hammerheads are bottom hunters that feed on lobsters, octopus and frequently, sting rays. Nearshore hammerheads are not particularly aggressive and only the largest ones have been implicated in human attacks. As with other sharks, Scalloped Hammerheads have been overexploited and should be released after capture.

Description: elongated body; gray to gray-green back with many small black spots; spade-shaped head; tall dorsal fin; elongated upper tail lobe

FISHING

Methods: still-fishing and drifting

Bait: crabs, cut or live fish

Where: bridges, docks and jetties

Tips: blue crabs are the best bait for Bonnetheads

BONNETHEAD
Sphyrna tiburo

Sphyrnidae

Other Names: bonnet or shovelnose shark

Habitat: shallows areas of saltier bays; sounds and estuaries; offshore during cold months

Food: primarily blue crabs, shrimp, squid and a few fish

Reproduction: matures at 2 to 3 years; 8 to 10 pups are born in late summer and early fall after a 5-month gestation period

Gulf Distribution: the entire Gulf; in the northern Gulf more common east of Mobile Bay

Average Size: 2 to 3 feet, 3 to 5 pounds

World Record: 26 pounds, Pounce Inlet, Florida, 2006

Table Quality: reportedly good but rarely eaten

Notes: The Bonnethead is the smallest and the most common species of hammerhead shark found in the Gulf. Bonnetheads are a shallow-water species that are often seen traveling in schools of 20 to a 100 or more fish. They are bottom feeders specializing on blue crabs, but they will also eat small fish and octopus. Like other sharks, Bonnetheads do not lay eggs but give birth to live young. The babies are about a foot long, almost $\frac{1}{3}$ the length of the mother. In the northern Gulf, Bonnetheads migrate offshore during the cooler months then re-enter the estuaries and bays in the spring.

149

Description: stout-bodied shark; short, broad, rounded
  snout; long front dorsal fin that begins above the middle
  of the pectoral fins; triangular upper teeth; no dermal ridge
  (ridge along the back)

FISHING

Methods: still-fishing and drifting

Bait: live fish, cut baits (particularly shark meat)

Where: mouth of coastal rivers, harbors and estuaries

Tips: fish the mouth of rivers and inlets with large baits

BULL SHARK

Carcharhinus leucas

Other Names: freshwater or river whaler, stubnosed shark

Habitat: midwater in bays, harbors and estuaries; well upstream freshwater rivers

Food: other sharks, mackerels, tuna, stingrays and crabs

Reproduction: matures at about 7 feet, then gives birth in summer to 6 to 8 live pups about 2½ feet long

Gulf Distribution: entire Gulf

Average Size: 6 to 8 feet, 100 to 200 pounds

World Record: 697 pounds, 12 ounces, Kenya, 2001

Table Quality: fair to good; sharks are marketed commercially in the Caribbean and South America where they are often grilled

Notes: The Bull Shark is one of the largest and most common sharks that is routinely found near shore in the Gulf of Mexico. A 490-pounder was caught off the Alabama coast. They are considered by some to be aggressive man-eaters and by others to be opportunistic feeders that only rarely mistake humans for prey. Their normal diet consists of large fish, frequently other sharks, that are captured well below the surface. Bull Sharks can withstand low salinity and on occasion travel far up coastal rivers. In Central America there are populations of landlocked Bull Sharks and records from the Mississippi River as far north as Illinois.

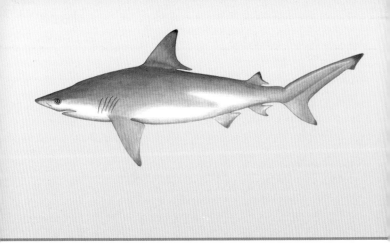

Description: elongated body; dark gray to gray-brown back; silver-white stripe on each side; long, pointed snout; black tips on all fins including the lower lobe of tail

FISHING

Methods: still-fishing, drifting and casting

Bait: live and cut fish, squid, lures

Where: bridges, party boats, small offshore boats

Tips: the best shark fishing is at dawn, dusk and throughout the night

BLACKTIP SHARK

Carcharhinus limbatus

Other Names: blacktip whaler, small and common blacktip shark, spinner or ground shark, sandshark, spotfin

Habitat: midwater in bays and estuaries out to open Gulf

Food: fish, small sharks, rays and squid

Reproduction: after a 10-month gestation period, 8 to 10 two-foot-long pups are born just offshore in early summer; pups then migrate to inshore waters

Gulf Distribution: the entire Gulf, one of the most common sharks in the northern Gulf

Average Size: 3 to 5 feet, 5 to 25 pounds

World Record: 270 pounds, 4 ounces, Kenya, 1984

Table Quality: one of the better-tasting sharks; often eaten in South America

Notes: Blacktip Sharks are one of the most common sharks in the Gulf of Mexico. This medium-sized shark is a midwater hunter that can be found from shallow bays and estuaries out to the open Gulf. Blacktips are very active, fast-swimming sharks that are known for jumping out of the water and spinning. This is one of the few sharks that will take artificial lures with any regularity and they are popular with fishermen on the flats, particularly fly fishermen.

Description: slender body with short, rounded snout; yellowish brown back with yellowish green sides; 2 dorsal fins of almost equal length; front dorsal fin begins behind pectoral fins

FISHING

Methods: casting, still-fishing and drifting

Bait: live and cut fish, lures and flies

Where: inshore shallows near mangroves and on flats, piers, docks and bridges

Tips: for all sharks, use a leader as long as the fish you expect to catch so the line isn't cut on the shark's rough hide

LEMON SHARK

Negaprion brevirostris

Carcharhinidae

Other Names: brown or yellow shark

Habitat: sea bottom in shallow inshore water out to about 60 feet; frequents flooded mangroves, grass flats and channels through the flats

Food: schooling fish, rays, squid and crabs

Reproduction: gives birth to 5 to 17 pups in shallow channels in early summer after a 12-month gestation period; pups are 24 to 26 inches long

Gulf Distribution: the entire Gulf; more common east of Mississippi River

Average Size: 4 to 6 feet, 15 to 25 pounds

World Record: 405 pounds, Buxton, North Carolina, 1988

Table Quality: good, but not often eaten; grilling with lots of lime juice is the best preparation for all shark meat

Notes: The Lemon Shark is a common shark in the warmer, shallow waters of the Gulf, out to about 60 feet deep. In warm weather they often rest on the bottom in small groups of 4 to 6 fish. In winter they gather in much larger schools of 100 fish or more. As with other sharks, these schools are often made up of fish of the same sex. Lemon sharks readily take lures and flies and are popular targets for fishermen of the flats. This is a large shark that has a nasty disposition and it should be approached and handled with caution.

Description: stout, colorful body with a very large mouth;
variable dark blotches and bars on paler body and fins;
3 vertical dark bars on tail

FISHING

Methods: still-fishing

Bait: live fish and shrimp, cut baits

Where: reefs, rocks near jetties and bridges

Tips: remove hook and release carefully

SPOTTED SCORPIONFISH

Scorpaena plumieri

Other Names: lionfish, rock scorpion

Habitat: primarily hides in holes in shallow reefs and wrecks but may be found in rocky areas near docks and jetties

Food: fish and crustaceans up to $1/2$ their body length

Reproduction: spawning occurs in the spring when eggs are laid in two hollow balloons that float to the surface then drift with the currents

Gulf Distribution: the entire Gulf, but much more common on southern reefs

Average Size: less than a pound

World Record: 3 pounds, 7 ounces, Brazil, 1997

Table Quality: excellent if large enough, but normally not worth the risk in preparation

Notes: The Spotted Scorpionfish is the only scorpionfish commonly found in the Gulf. On the East and West Coasts, some larger species of scorpionfish are prized as a food fish and are fished commercially. In the Gulf they are considered a venomous nuisance and they are not often large enough to risk cleaning. Their spines are venomous and painful, but not deadly. Scorpionfish hide in holes and ambush prey that can be almost half as long as they are.

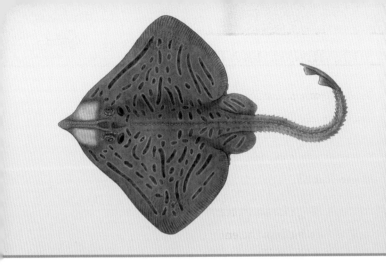

Description: flat body with a small tail fin; top reddish brown with dark, broken bars and a few dark spots; pointed snout with 2 clear spots on each side; 2 dorsal fins at the end of the tail are of nearly equal size; single row of short thorns along middle of back

FISHING

Methods: still-fishing

Bait: shrimp and cut bait

Where: any soft bottomed inshore waters

Tips: often found at mouth of muddy inlets

CLEARNOSE SKATE
Raja eglanteria

Other Names: window skate

Habitat: shallow coastal waters with a soft mud or sand bottom and high salinity; out to about 60 feet deep

Food: crustaceans and small bottom-dwelling fish

Reproduction: spawns in the shallows in early spring; eggs are laid in a horned oblong case with stiff tendrils at each corner; egg cases are often found on beaches

Gulf Distribution: the entire Gulf, but rare west of the Mississippi River

Average Size: 20 to 30 inches

World Record: none

Table Quality: probably edible, but not often eaten

Notes: Skates are often confused with stingrays but do not have a stinger on their tail and are harmless to humans. To distinguish a stingray from a skate, examine the tails. Skates have a thick tail and 2 dorsal fins close to the end of the tail. Rays have a long whip-like tail with no flattened end or top fins. Clearnose Skates are common in shallow, coastal waters during warmer months and are often caught in large numbers by anglers fishing the bottom. Skates are a harmless and beneficial part of the environment and should be returned to the water when caught.

Description: deep-bodied snapper; body brown with 8 pale vertical bars; all fins yellow; blue stripe under eye that may fade in older fish

FISHING

Methods: still-fishing and drifting

Bait: shrimp, live and cut fish

Where: rocky inshore water to deep reefs

Tips: small, brightly colored jigs tipped with shrimp or clam meat works well for these small snappers

SCHOOLMASTER
Lutjanus apodus

Lutjanidae

Other Names: barred or striped snapper

Habitat: small fish congregate near rocky inshore structure then move to offshore to wrecks and reefs as they grow larger

Food: small fish, squid and shrimp

Reproduction: spawning is in the late spring and early summer in shallow coastal waters

Gulf Distribution: entire Gulf

Average Size: less than a pound

World Record: none

Table Quality: excellent; small, but a great panfish when scaled and fried whole

Notes: The Schoolmaster is a small snapper that is found throughout the Gulf but is much more common on the reefs in Florida than further west. As the name suggests, Schoolmasters gather in schools and large clouds of them are often seen near wrecks and reef walls by divers. Small Schoolmasters (under a pound) stay inshore and are frequently caught from bridges and jetties. Both inshore and offshore, their abundance makes up for their small size. Schoolmasters are not only a good panfish for the skillet; they also make a good baitfish.

Description: narrow-bodied snapper; gray-green to brown body with reddish, coppery overtones; dark stripe from snout through eye; rounded anal fin

FISHING

Methods: still-fishing, drifting and casting

Bait: shrimp, live and cut fish and lures

Where: coastal channels and shallow bays out to the snapper banks

Tips: this is a skittish fish, so use long casts to fish edges of grass flats with a white jig tipped with a strip of cut fish

GRAY SNAPPER

Lutjanus griseus

Other Names: mangrove or black snapper

Habitat: near mangroves in shallow bays and estuaries out to wrecks and reefs down to about 300 feet

Food: fish, crabs and shrimp

Reproduction: spawns in midsummer in shallow bays at dusk under a full moon

Gulf Distribution: the entire Gulf, but more common and widespread in the southern Gulf

Average Size: 1 to 4 pounds

World Record: 17 pounds, Port Canaveral, Florida, 1992

Table Quality: excellent; smaller fish are good grilled or fried; large fish should be baked or poached

Notes: The Gray Snapper is a popular sport and commercial fish throughout its range. Gray Snappers are considered a shallow-water snapper but larger fish are more commonly found near reefs and wrecks in deep water out to about 300 feet. In shallow water, Gray Snappers are often found in flooded mangroves. These fish are wary and hard to catch in clear shallow water, but easy when there is cover. They are good fighters on light spinning tackle or a fly rod.

163

Description: rosy-red body with a greenish tint; sides have 8 to 10 yellow stripes and several vertical dark bars; a dark spot the size of the eye below the soft dorsal and above the lateral line; black edge on tail fin

FISHING

Methods: still-fishing, casting and drifting

Bait: shrimp, live and cut fish and lures

Where: offshore reefs and wrecks, docks, piers and jetties

Tips: fish a small Johnson spoon tipped with cut fish through deepwater grass

LANE SNAPPER

Lutjanus synagris

Other Names: candy or spot or red spot snapper

Habitat: from deep, clear water reefs and wrecks to brackish bays; mangrove shallows and grass flats

Food: feeds near the bottom on shrimp, worms, small crabs and fish

Reproduction: spawns in open water from spring through early fall; fry quickly move to grassy flats after hatching

Gulf Distribution: the entire Gulf; mainly offshore in the northern Gulf

Average Size: 8 to 12 inches and under a pound

World Record: 8 pounds, 3 ounces, Horseshoe Rigs, Mississippi, 2001

Table Quality: excellent; one of the best-tasting snappers when pan-fried

Notes: The Lane Snapper is a small snapper that can be found in many different habitats. They range from deep offshore reefs to shallow, murky estuaries. Unlike other snappers, they seem to prefer an open grassy bottom even when in deep water. In the southern Gulf they are often caught at the base of flooded mangroves. This small snapper has a delicate flavor and is a prized food fish throughout its range. In many areas it is commercially harvested.

Description: rosy red to pale red body fading to silver-red on lower sides; red fins; red eye; long pectoral fins; elongated anal fin

FISHING

> **Methods:** still-fishing and drifting
>
> **Bait:** squid, live and cut bait
>
> **Where:** offshore reefs and wrecks
>
> **Tips:** squid heads with long tentacles works very well for Red Snappers

RED SNAPPER

Lutjanus campechanus

Other Names: American or northern red snapper

Habitat: look for adults offshore in deep water (60 to 400 feet) over a hard bottom; young fish are found inshore over a hard bottom or over grass flats

Food: squid, shrimp, crustaceans and small fish

Reproduction: Red Snappers gather with grunts and other snappers to spawn from late spring through late summer; eggs are laid in open water just offshore; young move inshore

Gulf Distribution: the entire northern Gulf coast

Average Size: 1 to 5 pounds

World Record: 50 pounds, 4 ounces, Louisiana, 1996

Table Quality: world-class table fare as long as not overcooked

Notes: This North American fish is known around the world as an outstanding food fish and is highly sought after by commercial anglers and sport anglers alike. Most Red Snappers are caught well offshore on the "snapper banks" and you need a good boat to reach them. Snapper fishing from party boats is popular all along the Gulf Coast. Squid is a popular Red Snapper bait, but they can also be caught on cut bait. Both of these baits should be still-fished or moved very slowly just off the bottom.

Description: streamlined body; red body and fins fading to silver-pink sides; yellow stripes on sides; dorsal and anal fin margins are yellow-orange; no canine teeth; protruding lower jaw

FISHING

Methods: still-fishing and drifting

Bait: squid, shrimp and cut baits

Where: offshore reefs

Tips: Vermilions are best fished for at dawn and dusk

VERMILION SNAPPER
Rhomboplites aurorubens

Other Names: beeliner, scarlet snapper

Habitat: offshore reefs from 100 to 300 feet deep; nearshore breaks and walls 60 to 180 feet deep

Food: crabs, squid, shrimp and small fish

Reproduction: multiple spawning periods from spring through fall; free-floating eggs are released in deep, open water near shore

Gulf Distribution: offshore reefs in the northern Gulf; nearshore reefs and wrecks in the southern Gulf

Average Size: 1 to 1½ pounds

World Record: 7 pounds, 3 ounces, Mobile, Alabama, 1987

Table Quality: an excellent small snapper; the roe is also excellent

Notes: This is a small snapper that is often confused with the larger Red Snapper, and it is frequently marketed as Red Snapper. It's not hard to differentiate the two; the Red Snapper has prominent canine teeth and the Vermilion Snapper does not. The Vermilion Snapper is a midwater species and floats in schools above bottom structure. Light spinning tackle would be appropriate for this offshore panfish but most are caught on the same heavy boat rods used for other bottom-dwelling species. They are very good fighters on spinning tackle when a school is located in shallower nearshore waters.

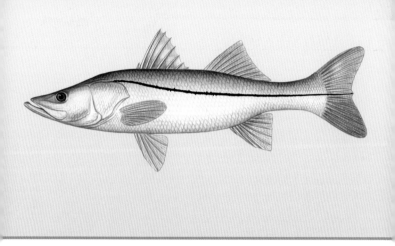

Description: elongated, streamlined body; silver with a tan or olive-brown tint; a flattened head with pointed snout and big mouth; distinct black lateral line; tall, separated dorsal fins

FISHING

Methods: casting, drifting and still-fishing

Bait: live fish, shrimp, lures and flies

Where: shallow mangrove channels

Tips: the best snook fishing is at night or on cloudy days a couple hours before high tide

COMMON SNOOK

Centropomus undecimalis

Other Names: saltwater or sea pike, linesider, robalo, sergeant fish

Habitat: shallow coastal waters with fast tide; flats and mangrove channels and into freshwater streams

Food: small fish, crabs and shrimp

Reproduction: spawns in midsummer in the mouths of passes and rivers; females may lay up to 50,000 eggs

Gulf Distribution: the southern Gulf, including Florida and southern Texas

Average Size: $1^{1}/_{2}$ to 3 feet

World Record: 53 pounds, 10 ounces, Costa Rica, 1978

Table Quality: one of the finest-tasting sport fish; best lightly broiled

Notes: The Common Snook is considered by many to be the premier marine game fish. They are available to anyone that can fish from a bridge, wade the shallows, or paddle a small boat. Snook are now popular with kayak fishermen. Snooks fight hard with spectacular, fast, hard runs and occasionally great leaps. Once landed, snook yield large flaky, white fillets with great flavor. The only downside to snook fishing is that they have been greatly overharvested and now are much less common than even a few years ago. Despite how good they taste, it's worth considering catch-and-release snook fishing.

171

Description: flattened body that is as deep as it is long; small mouth; silver body with 3 to 6 dark bands; anal and back dorsal fins are of a similar shape; long pelvic fin

FISHING

Methods: still-fishing and casting

Bait: shrimp, small cut baits

Where: piers, jetties and navigational buoys

Tips: suspended chum bags are very effective

ATLANTIC SPADEFISH

Chaetodipterus faber

Other Names: angelfish, striped or barred angelfish

Habitat: midwater near rocks or man-made structures in shallow coastal waters and out to near offshore reefs and wrecks

Food: a highly generalized feeder whose prey includes jellyfish, shrimp, crustaceans and fish

Reproduction: large schools of spawning fish gather around floating structure in midsummer; up to a million eggs are laid near the surface and hatch in a day or two

Gulf Distribution: the entire Gulf; more common in the northern Gulf

Average Size: 1 to 2 pounds

World Record: 14 pounds, Chesapeake Bay, Virginia, 1986

Table Quality: excellent flavor, but flesh has an unusual texture; fry small fish and bake larger ones; great in chowder

Notes: The spadefish is a common fish and is found in large schools around docks and jetties, but it is a hard fish to catch. Using a small hook will increase your chances of catching Spadefish. Spadefish have a small mouth and are adept at stealing bait from hooks. They often feed from midwater to the surface and respond well to floating chum bags. Small pieces of shrimp fished on a small hook and floated in the chum line can be very productive. Once hooked, they pull hard in a circle in an attempt to not leave the school.

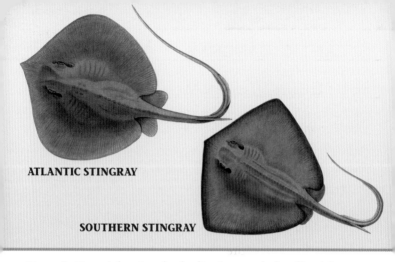

ATLANTIC STINGRAY

SOUTHERN STINGRAY

Description: Atlantic—body disc is rounded; yellowish-brown top; V-shaped snout; midline thorns present from eyes to spine; Southern—body disc is angular with sharp outer corners; brown to gray-green top; midline thorns present from eyes to base of tail

FISHING

Methods: still-fishing

Bait: shrimp and cut bait

Where: surf, docks and jetties, shallow flats

Tips: use a strong leader with sea urchin meat fished over a sandy bottom

174

ATLANTIC STINGRAY
Dasyatis sabina

SOUTHERN STINGRAY
Dasyatis americana

Other Names: stingaree

Habitat: common in bays and estuaries out to the coastal shelf (to 60 feet deep); readily enters freshwater streams

Food: crabs, clams, shrimp and small fish

Reproduction: eggs are reared within the female; 1 to 3 4-inch-long young are born alive

Gulf Distribution: entire Gulf

Average Size: 1 to 2 feet wide

World Record: Atlantic—10 pounds, 12 ounces; Galveston Bay, Texas, 1994; Southern—246 pounds, Galveston Bay, Texas, 1998

Table Quality: the flesh is very tasty and eaten in many countries, but not often in US

Notes: The Atlantic Stingray and the Southern Stingray are the common stingray species in the Gulf. The Atlantic Stingray is much smaller, often under a foot long, and has a very round shape. The Southern Stingray is much larger, commonly up to 100 pounds and is diamond-shaped. Both have a sharp spine on the tail that is venomous and can inflict a painful wound. Stingrays have strong grinding teeth that can easily crush even thick shells. Both stingrays hunt for prey while swimming along the bottom, and they also lie hidden in the sand with just their eyes showing. **175**

Description: slender body with a large head and pointed snout; olive-green or blue-gray back and silver sides; sides with 7 or 8 uninterrupted black stripes; 2 sharp points on gill cover

FISHING

Methods: casting, trolling and still-fishing

Bait: live fish, flies and lures

Where: large bays; river mouths

Tips: fish large white or silver surface plugs under flocking seagulls

STRIPED BASS
Morone saxatilis

Other Names: striper, streaker, surf bass, rockfish

Habitat: deep bays and coastal rivers; open sea and spawning streams on East Coast; introduced into some freshwater lakes and rivers in many Gulf States

Food: shad, menhaden and other small fish

Reproduction: ocean fish that enter freshwater streams to spawn; now hatchery-reared

Gulf Distribution: a few bays and river mouths on the northern Gulf coast

Average Size: 18 to 30 inches, 10 to 20 pounds

World Record: 78 pounds, 8 ounces, Atlantic City, New Jersey, 1982

Table Quality: excellent; small fish are good fried with a beer batter; large fish are best baked

Notes: The Striped Bass is the premier coastal sport fish in the Eastern US. They are not native to the Gulf States, but are now hatchery-reared and stocked in many freshwater lakes and large rivers. Striped Bass are becoming an important part of the freshwater sport fishery in many states. A few of these stocked fish move downstream to salt water and are being caught along the coast. There is no indication that any of these fish are breeding or on the way to becoming a self-supporting population.

Description: elongated body covered with armor-like scales;
slate-gray back and sides; long V-shaped snout; small
mouth under head

FISHING

This rare species is occasionally caught when fishing
the bottom both offshore and in rivers, but should
not be targeted. When a sturgeon is caught, it should
not be removed from the water. If it is not possible
to unhook the fish, the line should be cut a few
inches outside the mouth.

ATLANTIC STURGEON

Acipenseridae

Acipenser oxyrinchus

Other Names: none

Habitat: deep flats offshore, often near channels and river mouths; coastal spawning streams

Food: crustaceans and clams

Reproduction: migrates to brackish estuaries and up rivers to spawn, thousands of eggs are laid in moving water over gravel or sand to be fertilized a few at a time

Gulf Distribution: most common from the Mississippi River east

Average Size: 7 to 8 feet

World Record: none

Table Quality: oily, very good smoked; eggs eaten as caviar

Notes: Sturgeons are primitive fish with a history going back millions of years. Atlantic Sturgeons are bottom fish found along the coastal shelf in 60 to 200 feet of water during most of the year but they enter brackish or fresh water to spawn. Once extensively harvested commercially and by sport fishermen, they are now rare over most of their range and an endangered species in the Gulf. Atlantic Sturgeon are still occasionally caught by offshore or river anglers who frequently mistake them for sharks. Sturgeon are protected in all the Gulf States and should be released with care and reported to your state's natural resources agency.

Description: long, narrow body with small scales; greenish blue back and silver sides; small pointed head with a small terminal mouth; single dorsal fin begins just behind the start of pelvic fin; deeply forked tail

FISHING

> **Methods:** casting, still-fishing
>
> **Bait:** live fish, shrimp, flies and lures
>
> **Where:** shallow coastal water, streams and canals
>
> **Tips:** fish tidal inlets on a rising tide with a silver Rapala

LADYFISH
Elops saurus

Other Names: ten pounder, skipjack, bigeye herring, horse mackerel

Habitat: any shallow coastal waters; occasionally just off beaches and well up freshwater streams

Food: fish

Reproduction: spawns just offshore in late winter through early spring

Gulf Distribution: the entire Gulf

Average Size: 1 to 3 pounds

World Record: 8 pounds, Brazil, 2006

Table Quality: bony; not often eaten

Notes: Pound-for-pound this small relative of the Tarpon is one of the hardest-fighting fish to be found in the inshore waters of the Gulf. Common from just outside the beaches to shallow bays and well up freshwater streams, the Ladyfish would be a real prize if it had any food value at all. They are considered a nuisance by some, but when hooked in a channel on light spinning tackle or a fly rod, Ladyfish will test the skills of most anglers. Ladyfish and young Tarpon look very similar, but Ladyfish lack the long trailing filament on the dorsal fin.

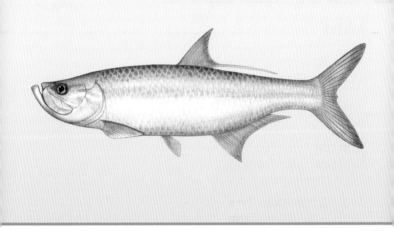

Description: long body covered with large plate-like scales; bluish green back and silver sides (fish from tannin stained water may be golden-bronze); large upturned mouth; last ray of dorsal fin very long

FISHING

Methods: casting, still-fishing, trolling and drifting

Bait: large live or dead fish, lures, flies, shrimp and crabs

Where: shallow flats, surf, channels and river mouths

Tips: fish large cut baits on the bottom at dawn and dusk

TARPON
Megalops atlanticus

Other Names: silver king

Habitat: shallow coastal waters and lower reaches of freshwater streams

Food: Fish, crabs, shrimp and octopus

Reproduction: Tarpons move offshore in May and June to spawn; young fish return to shallow streams and channels in a few weeks

Gulf Distribution: the southern Gulf all year long; the northern Gulf in warm weather

Average Size: 40 to 50 pounds

World Record: 283 pounds, Venezuela and Sierra Leone

Table Quality: not often eaten

Notes: Landlocked Tarpons are very common in Florida. In shallow coastal waters, the Tarpon is the king of game fish. They fight hard and make spectacular leaps. Smaller fish often dance on their tails more than the real giants do, but both put up a great show. Tarpon can tolerate a wide range of salinity levels, from the open seas to fresh water. In South America, there are even populations that are landlocked in freshwater lakes. These slow-growing fish are one of the most productive fish in the Gulf; large females may produce 12 million eggs. Despite this, their numbers seem to be decreasing in the northwestern Gulf and they are becoming uncommon to rare in Texas. Tarpons are highly regulated in many states and it takes a special license to keep one.

Description: deep body with concave forehead; variable color from tan or mottled brown to yellow-brown with dark blotches; rear dorsal and anal fins set far back near tail

FISHING

Methods: casting, drifting or still-fishing

Bait: shrimp or live fish

Where: near buoys, platforms and vegetation lines

Tips: nearshore Tripletails can be lured into anchored pine tree platforms

184

TRIPLETAIL
Lobotes surinamensis

Other Names: buoy fish or bass, blackfish, chobie, drift or leaf fish

Habitat: near floating surface structure from estuaries and bays to well offshore

Food: shrimp, small fish

Reproduction: little is known of the life history but gravid (egg-bearing) females are caught during the summer months and are often found in protected inshore waters

Gulf Distribution: entire Gulf

Average Size: 5 to 10 pounds

World Record: 42 pounds, 5 ounces, South Africa, 1989

Table Quality: reportedly very good; often baked

Notes: The Tripletail is a common fish often seen in many parts of the Gulf. It is frequently fished for in some regions but not in others. Tripletails are always found around some sort of floating structure, including buoys, boats or vegetation. They float or swim on their sides and resemble a piece of debris. Small Tripletails frequent the inshore bays and estuaries; larger fish are more commonly seen in deeper water. In fact, it is not uncommon to see large Tripletails in the open Gulf well offshore drifting beside vegetation lines. Once spotted, casting lures or flies can be very productive. When hooked, Tripletails are strong fighters and may need to be horsed away from the floating debris to keep them from becoming entangled.

Description: deep laterally compressed body with a steep forehead and a pointed snout; body is red to pink; forehead is dark; base of tail has a crescent; 3 long filaments on dorsal spines; dark spot at rear base of dorsal fin

FISHING

Methods: still-fishing, drifting, spear-fishing

Bait: clams, crabs, lobsters, shrimp and squid

Where: reefs and rock outcrops

Tips: hang a chum bag filled with crushed clams, crabs, lobster legs or shrimp shells and heads near a deep reef

HOGFISH

Lachnolaimus maximus

Other Names: hog snapper, hog wrasse

Habitat: deep coral reefs and rocks; shallower structure in South Florida

Food: crustaceans, mollusks and sea urchins

Reproduction: spawns in open water near deep reefs

Gulf Distribution: common in the warm southern Gulf; rare in the northern Gulf

Average Size: 2 to 5 pounds

World Record: 21 pounds, 6 ounces, Frying Pan Tower, South Carolina

Table Quality: excellent flavor and texture when fried or grilled

Notes: Hogfish are beautiful coral reef fish that are only common in the warmest Gulf waters. They are mostly associated with deeper reefs but in the Keys they are occasionally caught from bridges and other inshore structures. Hogfish are not strong fighters, but they make up what they lack in sporting abilities with their fine-flavored meat. Hogfish are popular targets for both line fisherman and divers, and in many areas their numbers have been greatly depleted.

GLOSSARY

adipose fin a small, fleshy fin without rays, located on the midline of the fish's back between the dorsal fin and the tail

air bladder a balloon-like organ located in the gut area of a fish, used to control buoyancy—and in the respiration of some species such as gar; also called "swim bladder" or "gas bladder"

anadromous saltwater fish that migrate into fresh water to spawn

anal fin a single fin located on the underside near the tail

annulus marks or rings on the scales, spine, vertebrae or otoliths that scientists use to determine a fish's age

anterior toward the front of a fish, opposite of posterior

bands horizontal markings running lengthwise along the side of a fish

barbel thread-like sensory structures on a fish's head often near the mouth, commonly called "whiskers"; used for taste or smell

bars vertical markings on the side of a fish

benthic organisms living in or on the bottom of a body of water

billfish marine fish with a spear or swordlike upper jaw, like the Blue Marlin

fingerling a juvenile fish, generally 1 to 10 inches in length, in its first year of life

fork length the overall length of fish from the mouth to the deepest part of the tail notch

blue water offshore ocean water

brood swarm a large group or "cloud" of young fish such as Black Bullheads

carnivore a predatory fish that feeds on other fish (also called a piscivore) or animals

catadromous a fish that lives in freshwater and migrates into saltwater to spawn, such as the American Eel

caudal fin the tail or tail fin

caudal peduncle the portion of the fish's body located between the anal fin and the beginning of the tail

copepod a small (less than 2 mm) crustacean, part of the zooplankton community

crustaceans a crayfish, water flea, crab or other animal belonging to group of mostly aquatic species that have paired antennae, jointed legs and an exterior skeleton (exoskeleton); common food for many fish

demersal aquatic animals that live near or on the seabed

dorsal relating to the top of the fish, on or near the back; opposite of the ventral, or lower, part of the fish

dorsal fin the fin or fins located along the top of a fish's back

estuary protected coastal waters that are often brackish

eddy a circular water current, often created by an obstruction

exotic a foreign species, not native to a watershed, such as the Zebra Mussel

fingerling a juvenile fish, generally 1 to 10 inches in length, in its first year of life

finlet small individual fins on fast swimming fish

fork length the overall length of fish from mouth to the deepest part of the tail notch

fry recently hatched young fish that have already absorbed their yolk sacs

game fish a species regulated by laws for recreational fishing

gills organs used in aquatic respiration (breathing)

gill cover large bone covering the fish's gills, also called opercle or operculum

gill flap also called ear flap; fleshy projection on the back edge of the gill cover of some fish such as Bluegill

gill raker a comb-like projection from the gill arch

harvest fish that are caught and kept by recreational or commercial anglers

ichthyologist a scientist who studies fish

invertebrates animals without backbones, such as insects, leeches and earthworms

lateral line a series of pored scales along the side of a fish that contain organs used to detect vibrations and water currents

littoral shoreline area

mandible lower jaw

maxillary upper jaw

mollusk an invertebrate with a smooth, soft body such as a clam or a snail, often having an outer shell

native an indigenous or naturally occurring species

omnivore a fish or animal that eats plants and animal matter

otolith calcium concentration found in the inner ear of fish; used to determine age of some fish; also called ear bone

opercle the bone covering the gills, also called the gill cover or operculum

panfish small freshwater game fish that can be fried whole in a pan

pectoral fins paired fins on the side of the fish located just behind the gills

pelagic fish species that live in open water, in the food-rich upper layer of the column; not associated with the bottom

pelvic fins paired fins located below or behind the pectoral fins on the bottom (ventral portion) of the fish

pharyngeal teeth teeth in the throat of fish used for grinding

piscivore a predatory fish that mainly eats other fish

planktivore a fish that feeds on plankton

plankton floating or weakly swimming aquatic plants and animals, including larval fish, that drift with the current; often eaten by fish; individual organisms are called plankters

range the geographic region in which a species is found

ray hard stiff fin support; resembles a spine but is jointed

ray soft flexible fin support, sometimes branched

roe fish eggs

scales small, flat plates covering the outer skin of many fish

shoal shallow water or school of fish

silt small, easily disturbed bottom particles smaller than sand but larger than clay

siltation the accumulation of soil particles

spawning the process of fish reproduction; involves females laying eggs and males fertilizing them to produce young fish

spine stiff, non-jointed structures found along with soft rays in some fins

spiracle an opening on the posterior portion of the head above and behind the eye

standard length length of the fish from the mouth to the end of the vertebral column

stocking the purposeful, artificial introduction of a fish species into a body of water

substrate bottom composition of a lake, stream or river

subtenninal mouth a mouth below the snout of the fish

swim bladder see air bladder

tailrace area of water immediately downstream of a dam or power plant

terminal mouth forward facing

total length length of fish from the mouth to the tail compressed to its fullest length

turbid cloudy; water clouded by suspended sediments or plant matter that limits visibility and the passage of light

vent the opening at the end of the digestive tract

ventral the underside of the fish

vertebrate an animal with a backbone

yolk the part of an egg containing food for the developing fish

zooplankton the animal component of plankton; tiny animals that float or swim weakly; common food for small fish

REFERENCES

Dickson Hoese, H., Moore, R.H., and Calhoun, A.F.
Fishes of the Gulf of Mexico
Texas A&M University Press, 1998

Dunaway, V.
Sport Fish of the Gulf of Mexico
Florida Sportsman, 2008

McClane, A.J.
Field Guide to Saltwater Fishes of North America
Henry Holt and Company, 1974

Parsons, G.R.
Shark, Skates and Rays of the Gulf of Mexico
University Press of Mississippi, 2006

Robins, R.C., and Ray, G.C.
A Field Guide to Atlantic Coast Fishes
Houghton Mifflin Company, 1986

Schultz, K.
Field Guide to Saltwater Fish
John Wiley & Sons, Inc., 2004

Shipp, R.L.
Dr. Bob Shipp's Guide to the Fishes of the Gulf of Mexico
Marine Environmental Science Consortium, 1986

Walls, J.G.
Fishes of the Northern Gulf of Mexico, 1975

INDEX

194

ABOUT THE AUTHOR

Dave Bosanko was born in Kansas and studied engineering before following his love of nature to degrees in biology and chemistry from Emporia State University. He spent thirty years as staff biologist at two of the University of Minnesota's field stations. Though his training was in mammal physiology, Dave worked on a wide range of research projects ranging from fish, bird and mammal population studies to experiments with biodiversity and prairie restoration. A lifelong fisherman and avid naturalist, he is now spending his retirement writing, fishing and traveling.